Distribution from Large Terrorist Attacks Under the Terrorism Risk Insurance Act

Stephen J. Carroll, Tom LaTourrette, Brian G. Chow,
Gregory S. Jones, Craig Martin

CENTER FOR TERRORISM
RISK MANAGEMENT POLICY

The research described in this report was conducted by the RAND Center for Terrorism Risk Management Policy.

Library of Congress Cataloging-in-Publication Data

Distribution of losses from large terrorist attacks under the Terrorism Risk Insurance
  Act / Stephen J. Carroll ... [et al.].
    p. cm.
    "MG-427."
    Includes bibliographical references.
    ISBN 0-8330-3865-6 (pbk. : alk. paper)
    1. Insurance, Casualty—Law and legislation—United States. 2. Risk
  management—United States. 3. Terrorism—United States. I. Carroll, Stephen J.,
  1940– II. RAND Center for Terrorism Risk Management Policy.

  KF1215.D57 2005
  346.73'0861—dc22

                                                                    2005029744

The RAND Corporation is a nonprofit research organization providing objective analysis and effective solutions that address the challenges facing the public and private sectors around the world. RAND's publications do not necessarily reflect the opinions of its research clients and sponsors.

RAND® is a registered trademark.

© Copyright 2005 RAND Corporation

All rights reserved. No part of this book may be reproduced in any form by any electronic or mechanical means (including photocopying, recording, or information storage and retrieval) without permission in writing from RAND.

Published 2005 by the RAND Corporation
1776 Main Street, P.O. Box 2138, Santa Monica, CA 90407-2138
1200 South Hayes Street, Arlington, VA 22202-5050
201 North Craig Street, Suite 202, Pittsburgh, PA 15213-1516
RAND URL: http://www.rand.org/
To order RAND documents or to obtain additional information, contact
Distribution Services: Telephone: (310) 451-7002;
Fax: (310) 451-6915; Email: order@rand.org

The RAND Center for Terrorism Risk Management Policy (CTRMP)

The CTRMP provides research that is needed to inform public and private decisionmakers on economic security in the face of the threat of terrorism. Terrorism risk insurance studies provide the backbone of data and analysis to inform appropriate choices with respect to the renewal of the Terrorism Risk Insurance Act (TRIA) in 2005. Research on the economics of various liability decisions informs the policy decisions of the U.S. Congress and the opinions of state and federal judges. Studies of compensation help Congress to ensure that appropriate compensation is made to the victims of terrorist attacks. Research on security helps to protect critical infrastructure and to improve collective security in rational and cost-effective ways.

The CTRMP is housed at the RAND Corporation, an international nonprofit research organization with a reputation for rigorous and objective analysis and the world's leading provider of research on terrorism. The center combines three organizations:

- RAND Institute for Civil Justice, which brings a 25-year history of empirical research on liability and compensation.
- RAND Infrastructure, Safety and Environment, which conducts research on homeland security and public safety.
- Risk Management Solutions, the world's leading provider of models and services for catastrophe risk management.

An advisory board helps identify important policy questions and priority research areas. The research portfolio of the CTRMP is developed through a competitive proposal process within RAND. For additional information about the Center for Terrorism Risk Management Policy, contact:

Robert Reville
RAND Corporation
1776 Main Street
P.O. Box 2138
Santa Monica, CA 90407
Robert_Reville@rand.org
(310) 393-0411, Ext. 6786

Debra Knopman
RAND Corporation
1200 South Hayes Street
Arlington, VA 22202-5050
Debra_Knopman@rand.org
(703) 413-1100, Ext. 5667

A profile of the CTRMP, abstracts of its publications, and ordering information can be found at http://www.rand.org/multi/ctrmp/.

Center for Terrorism Risk Management Policy Advisory Board

Jeffrey D. DeBoer (Co-Chair)
President & Chief Executive Officer
Real Estate Roundtable

Jacques Dubois (Co-Chair)
Chairman
Swiss Re America Holding Corporation

Jack D. Armstrong
Assistant Vice President and
*   Senior Regulatory Counsel*
Liberty Mutual Insurance Company

Kim M. Brunner, Esq.
Executive Vice President and
*   General Counsel*
State Farm Insurance

Andrew Coburn
Chief Knowledge Architect
Risk Management Solutions, Inc.

Kenneth R. Feinberg, Esq.
Managing Partner
The Feinberg Group, LLP

John Gorte
Executive Vice President
Dorinco/Dow Chemical

Ken Jenkins
Senior Vice President
Corporate Underwriting/Risk Management
American Reinsurance

Peter Lowy
Chief Executive Officer
Westfield Corporation, Inc.

James Macdonald
Executive Vice President and
*   Chief Underwriting Officer*
ACE USA

Kathleen Nelson
Immediate Past Chair
International Council of Shopping
*   Centers (ICSC)*

Art Raschbaum
General Director, Corporate Risk
*   Management and Insurance*
General Motors Corporation

Hemant Shah
President and Chief Executive Officer
Risk Management Solutions, Inc.

Cosette R. Simon
Senior Vice President for Government
*   and Industry Relations*
Swiss Re Life & Health America Inc.

Steven A. Wechsler
President and Chief Executive Officer
National Association of Real Estate
*   Investment Trusts*

Preface

The pending expiration of the Terrorism Risk Insurance Act (TRIA) requires that policymakers assess the effectiveness of TRIA and decide whether to extend, modify, or terminate it. To help inform the debate over the future of TRIA, this study examines how losses from large terrorist attacks would be distributed to various parties under TRIA. The study also examines how losses would be distributed under various possible modifications of TRIA. The results are intended to help policymakers understand how TRIA and various alternatives might perform in practice and to evaluate the extent to which the shared costs of recovery from a terrorist attack would be distributed equitably.

The primary audience for this work is decisionmakers in Congress and the U.S. Departments of the Treasury and Homeland Security. The work is intended to inform these decisionmakers about some quantitative ramifications of TRIA in the event of specific large terrorist attack scenarios. Such information should help guide thinking about terrorism insurance options in light of TRIA's pending expiration. In addition, this work should help commercial insurers and policyholders understand the implications of terrorist attacks for their respective industries in light of TRIA.

This research was funded by CTRMP, which is a partnership between RAND and Risk Management Solutions, Inc. CTRMP is funded by voluntary contributions from several organizations that represent property owners and other insurance purchasers, reinsurers, and insurers. An advisory board that included representatives of the donor organizations was invited to comment on the book, but the scope, analytical methods, conclusions, and recommendations were determined solely by RAND.

This book is the third on terrorism insurance published by CTRMP. The first, *Issues and Options for Government Intervention in the Market for Terrorism Insurance* (Dixon et al., 2004), reviewed the literature on terrorism insurance and discussed the policy issues and options for change. The second, *Trends in Terrorism: Threats to the United States and the Future of the Terrorism Risk Insurance Act* (Chalk et al., 2005) examined the implications of recent trends in domestic and foreign terrorism for policy related to terrorism insurance in the United States. These books are available at http://www.rand.org/multi/ctrmp/.

Contents

Figures

Tables

Summary

Introduction

Following the 9/11 attacks and the substantial losses incurred, insurers questioned their ability to pay claims in future attacks and began to exclude terrorism coverage from commercial insurance policies. The fear that a lack of insurance coverage would threaten economic stability and growth, urban development, and jobs led the federal government to adopt the Terrorism Risk Insurance Act (TRIA) of 2002. TRIA's purpose is twofold: (1) protect consumers by addressing market disruptions and ensure the continued widespread availability and affordability of property and casualty insurance for terrorism risk; and (2) allow for a transitional period for the private markets to stabilize, resume pricing of such insurance, and build capacity to absorb any future losses.

Because TRIA sunsets at the end of 2005, policymakers need to assess how TRIA, as currently written, will respond to the losses that might result from different modes and magnitudes of terrorist attacks. In particular, in assessing TRIA, policymakers must decide if TRIA's likely effects on the distribution of losses resulting from a terrorist attack are satisfactory and, if not, what changes to TRIA, including its termination, would be needed to improve its performance.

Because there have been no large terrorist attacks in the United States since TRIA came into effect, policymakers have little empirical data on which to base an assessment of the likely effects of TRIA. This study is designed to provide policymakers with empirical estimates of TRIA's likely effects on the distribution of losses resulting from a terrorist attack. We generate a database by simulating the expected losses for different sizes and modes of terrorist attack scenarios—in particular, crashing a hijacked aircraft into a major building, releasing anthrax within a major building, and releasing anthrax outdoors in a major urban area—and then examine the effects of the insurance system and TRIA on the ultimate distribution of the losses under different circumstances.

Estimating Losses from a Large Terrorist Attack

To provide an accurate basis on which to determine the effects of TRIA, we simulate the expected losses and the distribution of losses across insurance lines for a number of attack scenarios of each of the three attack modes noted above. The attack modes selected represent feasible attacks and indeed were chosen because they involve methods (aircraft impact) or materials (anthrax) that have been used in previous terrorist attacks. They also represent a range of potential outcomes and, therefore, can provide some information on the robustness of TRIA.

Tables S.1 and S.2 illustrate the estimates generated from the simulations in terms of casualty distributions and losses by insurance line, respectively, for the three example scenarios. Table S.1, which categorizes by casualty type, shows that an outdoor anthrax attack leads to the largest number of casualties (more than two million), with over 36,000 deaths. This extreme catastrophic scenario exceeds the size of the other two scenarios by an order of magnitude; as such, the scenario is useful in illustrating the performance of TRIA in an attack far larger than 9/11. The indoor anthrax attack leads to the smallest number of casualties, although with greater severity: Serious injuries and fatalities both exceed the aircraft impact attack.

Table S.2 shows that the distribution of losses among insurance lines varies across the three example scenarios. Property losses account for 13 percent of the total loss in the indoor anthrax scenario, 58 percent of the total in the outdoor anthrax scenario, and 67 percent of

Table S.1
Casualty Distributions for Terrorist Attack Scenarios

Casualty Type	Aircraft Impact (Major Office Building)	Indoor Anthrax (Major Office Building)	Outdoor Anthrax (Major Urban Area)
Medical only	35,524	5,500	1,901,476
Temporary total disability	641	1,500	19,960
Permanent partial disability— minor	561	—	—
Permanent partial disability— major	401	—	—
Permanent total disability	430	4,500	59,881
Fatal	2,632	2,750	36,594
Total	40,188	14,250	2,017,911

Table S.2
Allocation of Losses by Insurance Line for Terrorist Attack Scenarios (in millions of dollars)

Insurance Line	Aircraft Impact (Major Office Building)	Indoor Anthrax (Major Office Building)	Outdoor Anthrax (Major Urban Area)
Property	$4,482	$1,061	$100,414
Workers' compensation	$1,522	$6,115	$43,472
Group life	$307	$323	$2,472
Individual life	$235	$247	$2,109
Accidental death and dismemberment	$121	$208	$1,483
Health	$1	$10	$22,354
Total	$6,668	$7,964	$172,304

the total in the aircraft impact scenario. Workers' compensation shows a complementary variation, accounting for 77 percent of the losses in indoor anthrax, 25 percent in outdoor anthrax, and 23 percent in aircraft impact. Life and health lines entail 10 percent in the indoor anthrax and aircraft impact scenarios and 16 percent in the outdoor anthrax scenario.

The Distribution of Terrorism Attack Losses Under TRIA

TRIA requires primary insurers to make terrorism coverage available to commercial policyholders. In return for making coverage available, TRIA limits the amount that insurers are responsible for paying by means of a risk-sharing formula. In this formula, a primary insurer is responsible for paying losses it insured up to an annual deductible and for a co-payment of all losses above the deductible. Insured losses above the deductible and co-payment are paid by a surcharge on all commercial insurance policyholders and by taxpayers.

TRIA applies to commercial property and casualty policies only; it does not apply to life or health policies or to personal lines such as auto or homeowners' insurance. In addition, TRIA is restricted to certified foreign terrorist attacks only; TRIA does not apply to domestic terrorist attacks. Finally, TRIA allows insurers to exclude property losses from chemical, biological, radiological, and nuclear (CBRN) incidents from policies as long as the exclusion is also applied to losses arising from events other than acts of terrorism. Workers' compensation losses cannot be excluded from any terrorism insurance policy. Losses from a CBRN attack that are insured are eligible for the risk-spreading provision of TRIA.

Figure S.1 illustrates TRIA's general features. Certain parameters of TRIA change from year to year; the figure shows TRIA's 2005 parameters.

The left part of the figure shows the distribution of initial payouts under TRIA. Target insurers who have paid claims on policies that include terrorism coverage and are in lines eligible for TRIA coverage (here referred to as TRIA-covered losses) are responsible for payouts up to an annual deductible equal to 15 percent (in 2005) of the insurer's group's annual direct-earned premium on TRIA-eligible lines the previous year. A target insurer is also responsible for a co-payment of 10 percent of all losses above the deductible. The remaining 90 percent of losses above the deductible are reimbursed to the insurer by the federal government. This formula is applied for aggregate annual insured losses in TRIA-eligible lines up to $100 bil-

Figure S.1
Summary of Initial and Final Payouts Under TRIA

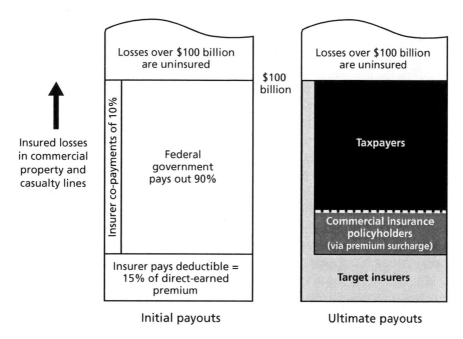

lion. TRIA specifies that insurers are not responsible for TRIA-covered losses above $100 billion, but it does not explicitly specify who would be responsible for insured losses in excess of $100 billion.

TRIA also requires that the federal government recoup the difference between an "insurance marketplace aggregate retention amount" ($15 billion in 2005) and the sum of insurer deductibles and co-payments for that year. Recoupment is collected through a surcharge of up to 3 percent per year on all commercial insurance policies in the United States. The right part of the figure shows the ultimate distribution of payouts after recoupment.

TRIA formally distributes the losses resulting from a terrorist attack among five groups: (1) people and businesses who lack coverage for terrorism losses and must, therefore, bear the losses themselves (here referred to as "uninsured"); (2) insurers of losses covered by policies in insurance lines not eligible for TRIA coverage (here referred to as "life and health insurers"); (3) insurers of losses covered by policies in commercial insurance lines that are eligible for TRIA coverage (here referred to as "target insurers"); (4) all commercial insurance policyholders in the country, from whom the federal government recoups all or part of its initial payout (here referred to as "commercial policyholders"), and (5) taxpayers. Five provisions of the law—insurance availability and take-up, TRIA eligibility, deductibles and co-payments, insurance marketplace retention, and the ceiling on insurers' responsibility—determine how the losses resulting from a terrorist attack are redistributed among these five groups.

Figure S.2 shows how cumulative annual losses resulting from each mode of attack would generally be distributed under TRIA. Total losses for single attacks from the three example scenarios discussed above are indicated by an arrow on the horizontal axis for each of the three attack types in Figure S.2. Distributions are shown as a function of cumulative annual losses because target insurers' deductible and co-payment under TRIA are applied to annual losses. If an insurer suffers losses from multiple events in a single year, these losses are combined to determine when the TRIA deductible has been met. Each curve in Figure S.2 shows the portion of the total annual loss that would be paid by various stakeholders, assuming current take-up values.

Uninsured losses, which represent a constant fraction of the total loss in all cases, vary considerably with the attack mode, but they would be substantial in all cases, ranging from 13 percent of the total loss for indoor anthrax attacks to 57 percent of the total loss for outdoor anthrax attacks. Less than 3 percent of commercial policyholders purchase CBRN coverage for property losses. However, in the indoor anthrax case, the majority of losses come from workers' compensation, for which CBRN coverage is mandatory; so the overall uninsured loss fraction is relatively small. By contrast, the outdoor anthrax scenario would have a much higher proportion of property losses; hence, the low take-up for these lines would result in a high fraction of the loss going uninsured.

Figure S.2
TRIA Loss Distributions for Cumulative Annual Losses Resulting from Different Types of Terrorist Attacks

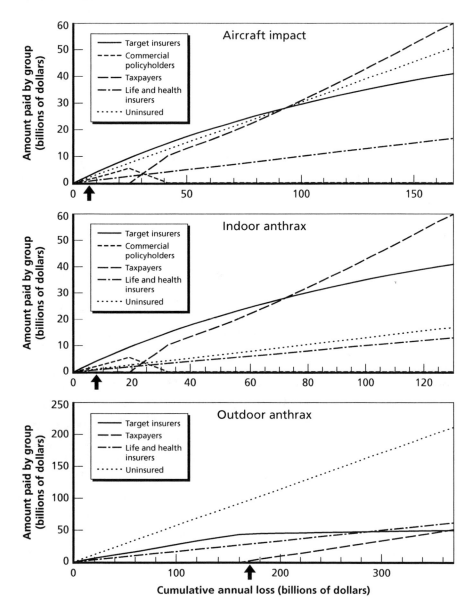

Losses for life and health insurers represent a constant fraction of the total loss, ranging from 10 percent in the aircraft impact and indoor anthrax scenarios to 16 percent in the outdoor anthrax scenario. Because they are not eligible for TRIA, losses in life and health lines would be the insurers' responsibility.

Losses to property insured against terrorism and workers' compensation losses qualify for the risk-spreading provisions of TRIA and would be shared by target insurers, commercial policyholders, and taxpayers. Because aircraft impact and indoor anthrax attacks would be concentrated around a single target building, while losses in an outdoor anthrax attack would be dispersed over hundreds or even thousands of sites, loss distributions in aircraft impact and indoor anthrax attacks have different characteristics than the distribution in an outdoor anthrax attack.

In the aircraft impact and indoor anthrax scenarios, target insurers would pay the largest share of losses (through the aggregate deductible and co-payment) up to a total loss of approximately $75 billion–$95 billion. For a $50 billion annual loss, target insurers would pay $17 billion for aircraft impact attacks and $21 billion for indoor anthrax attacks. TRIA's loss-sharing formula is such that TRIA-covered losses beyond the target insurers' share are paid by commercial policyholders up to a total loss of $25 billion–$30 billion and by taxpayers above that (see Figure S.2). Above a total loss of $75 billion–$95 billion, taxpayers pay the largest share of the loss.

The loss distribution for outdoor anthrax releases is very different. There, the insured losses are expected to be spread among the vast majority of property/casualty insurers in the country. This assumption, in conjunction with the low fraction of losses that would be insured, leads to a situation in which target insurers receive no reimbursement for claims payments until the total loss exceeds $164 billion. At this point the TRIA-covered loss equals the total commercial insurance industry-wide deductible of $44 billion. For total losses greater than $164 billion, all target insurers will have met their deductibles and taxpayers would begin to contribute. TRIA-covered losses paid by target insurers in an outdoor anthrax attack would exceed the insurance marketplace retention; there would be no surcharge and general commercial policyholders do not contribute to the losses. Losses would be shared entirely by target insurers and taxpayers.

A significant finding is that taxpayers would pay nothing in a single attack for any of the scenarios examined. In the aircraft impact and indoor anthrax scenarios, taxpayers would pay nothing because the loss ($6 billion–$8 billion; see arrows on the horizontal axes in Figure S.2) would be within the loss range under which the federal government recoups all its initial payout through the commercial policyholder surcharge. In fact, even the World Trade Center attacks would not have required a taxpayer contribution had TRIA been in place. In general, for attacks concentrated on a single target, which would include bombs, aircraft impacts, or indoor biological or chemical attacks, at least three to four very large attacks would need to occur in a year before taxpayers would begin to contribute.

In the outdoor anthrax release scenario, taxpayers would pay nothing because losses would be spread among so many target insurers that few would meet their deductible; hence, the federal government would never even make an initial payout. Note, however, that the total loss in our example simulation is just below the point at which taxpayers would begin to contribute.

Our results show that the ultimate distribution of losses under TRIA depends on the attack mode and cumulative annual losses. The results shown in Figure S.2 illustrate that TRIA creates multiple regimes that differ in terms of the parties' relative shares of terrorism losses—regimes that are summarized in Table S.3.

Uninsured building and business owners and life and health insurers pay part of any loss and so contribute over the entire loss interval. TRIA does not take effect until the TRIA-covered losses reach $5 million, so insurers on sites incurring losses (target insurers) pay the entire loss up to this point. Assuming current terrorism insurance take-up, we estimate that TRIA-covered losses will reach $5 million when total losses in aircraft impact attacks reach $8.5 million or total losses in indoor anthrax attacks reach $6.5 million.

Table S.3
TRIA Loss Distribution Regimes

Who Pays		Total Loss Interval (at current take-up)		
		Aircraft Impact	Indoor Anthrax	Outdoor Anthrax
Uninsured + life and health	Target	$0–$8.5M	$0–$6.5M	$0–$164B
	Target + commercial	$8.5M–$25B	$6.5M–$20B	—
	Target + commercial + taxpayer	$25B–$43B	$20B–$33B	—
	Target + taxpayer	$43B–$167B	$33B–$130B	$164B–$370B
	Unspecified	>$167B	>$130B	>$370B

NOTES: Uninsured = people and businesses who lack coverage for terrorism losses; life and health = insurers of losses in life and health lines, which are not eligible for TRIA coverage; target = insurers of losses covered by policies in commercial insurance lines eligible for TRIA coverage; commercial = all commercial policyholders in the country. M = millions. B = billions.

When total losses exceed these respective values, commercial policyholders begin contributing. Commercial policyholders do not contribute in the outdoor anthrax case and target insurers pay the entire loss up to $164 billion.

In the aircraft impact and indoor anthrax cases, taxpayers begin to contribute once the TRIA-covered loss reaches the $15 billion insurance marketplace aggregate retention amount. We estimate that, on average, this would occur at a total annual loss of about $25 billion ($20 billion) for aircraft impact (indoor anthrax) attacks.

Commercial policyholders cease to contribute once the aggregate deductible plus co-payment reaches the $15 billion retention. We estimate that, on average, deductibles and co-payments would reach the retention at a total loss of about $43 billion ($33 billion) for aircraft impact (indoor anthrax) attacks.

Finally, the responsibility for payment of TRIA-covered losses above the $100 billion program cap are unspecified. This corresponds to total losses of $167 billion ($130 billion) for aircraft impact (indoor anthrax) attacks and $370 billion for outdoor anthrax attacks.

Loss Distributions Under Potential Modifications to TRIA

Some observers might object to one or another aspect of the distributions accomplished by TRIA, believing that some group could be allocated an inappropriate share under certain circumstances, such as particular modes or sizes of terrorist attacks. Others might believe that the distributions accomplished by the current TRIA might fail to achieve TRIA's objective of maintaining a viable terrorism insurance market. In either case, TRIA would have to be modified to change the loss distribution.

To help elucidate the effects of various possible modifications to TRIA on the overall loss distribution, we estimate the loss distribution that would result when the different provisions of TRIA are changed. In each case, we begin with a loss distribution goal and then estimate the effect through simulation of some possible modifications to TRIA in achieving this goal. Table S.4 summarizes the results, which are described below. The key point is that losses are fixed. This means that any attempts to shift distribution goals will not reduce losses; they will simply shift the burden from one group to another group or groups.

Reduce Uninsured Losses

By design, TRIA helps reduce uninsured terrorism losses in two ways: by mandating that insurers offer coverage for certain losses resulting from terrorist attacks and by limiting the amount that insurers are responsible for paying, thereby allowing premiums to be lower than they would be without TRIA. Two possible modifications that may help further reduce the uninsured losses in a terrorist attack are extending the "make-available" requirement for terrorism insurance to include CBRN coverage and making terrorism insurance coverage

Table S.4
Distribution of Losses Under Possible Modifications to TRIA

Loss Distribution Goal	Possible Modifications	Where Losses Are Transferred
Reduce uninsured losses	Mandate CBRN coverage availability Make terrorism insurance coverage mandatory	Target insurers, commercial policyholders, and taxpayers
Reduce burden on target insurers	Decrease insurer deductibles	Commercial policyholders or taxpayers
Reduce burden on commercial policyholders	Increase insurer deductibles Decrease insurance marketplace retention	Target insurers Taxpayers
Reduce burden on taxpayers	Increase the deductible and/or insurance marketplace retention Decrease TRIA ceiling	Target insurers or commercial policyholders Unknown

mandatory in commercial insurance policies. Reductions in uninsured losses will result in increased losses to target insurers, commercial policyholders, and taxpayers.

A potential drawback of requiring insurers to offer CBRN coverage is that it could leave individual target insurers more vulnerable to losses that exceed their payment capacity. The principal concern among insurers is that damage from a CBRN attack could span a very large geographic area and a long time duration. This concern is exacerbated by the limited availability of reinsurance for terrorism. While the loss-sharing provision of TRIA acts as reinsurance, TRIA provides less flexibility for an insurer to tailor the amount of reinsurance it obtains in different markets (e.g., different geographic areas or insurance lines) than does commercial reinsurance.

Reduce Burden on Target Insurers

If a goal was to reduce the burden on the target insurers, the insurer deductible or co-payment must be reduced. Because in most situations an insurer's deductible will be much greater than its co-payment, a decrease in the deductible has a greater effect than an equivalent percentage decrease in the co-payment. Decreasing the insurer deductible was proposed by Chalk et al. (2005) to reduce terrorism insurance premiums and increase coverage take-up without increasing the burden on taxpayers. This could be a viable approach, but the burden on taxpayers would be unchanged only for losses below the insurance marketplace retention amount. For a loss above the retention amount, any reduction in losses for target insurers is offset by increased losses to taxpayers.

Reduce Burden on Commercial Policyholders

The burden on taxpayers can be reduced by increasing the deductible and/or the insurance marketplace retention. Either will shift losses from taxpayers to target insurers or commercial policyholders or both, depending on the size of the loss. The burden on taxpayers could also be reduced by decreasing the aggregate ceiling on TRIA loss sharing. A reduction in the ceiling will reduce taxpayers' responsibility for extremely large losses. However, the law, as currently written, leaves open the determination of whether TRIA-covered losses in excess of $100 billion will be paid and, if so, by whom. Consequently, it is not known who would become responsible for losses shifted from taxpayers.

Reduce Burden on Taxpayers

The burden on taxpayers can be reduced either by increasing the deductible and/or the insurance marketplace retention or decreasing the aggregate ceiling on TRIA loss sharing. Either can shift losses from taxpayers to target insurers or commercial policyholders or both, depending on the size of the loss. A reduction in the ceiling will reduce taxpayers' responsibility for extremely large losses. However, the law, as currently written, leaves open the determination of whether TRIA-covered losses in excess of $100 billion will be paid and, if so, by whom. Consequently, it is not known who would become responsible for losses shifted from taxpayers.

Conclusions and Implications for TRIA

In terms of the conclusions, we focus on four areas: (1) the taxpayer role under TRIA, (2) uninsured losses under TRIA, (3) target insurer subsidy, and (4) the renewal of TRIA.

Taxpayer Role Under TRIA

Based on our analysis, we concluded that, overall, the role of taxpayers is expected to be minimal in all but very rare cases, such as serial large attacks on major buildings, highly effective large outdoor anthrax releases, or nuclear detonations. An important conclusion from this finding is that TRIA is not primarily a taxpayer bailout of the insurance industry.

An implication of this conclusion is that alternatives to TRIA need not focus on protecting taxpayers. Thus, alternatives designed to reduce the burden on taxpayers (increasing the deductible and/or the insurance marketplace retention and decreasing the TRIA ceiling) do not need to be high priorities. In addition, deliberations over other TRIA alternatives should discount potential adverse effects on taxpayers, as long as the alternatives do not significantly decrease the point at which taxpayers begin to contribute.

It should also be noted that, even in cases where taxpayers ultimately pay nothing under the TRIA loss distribution formula, there is some indirect effect on taxpayers. First, some fraction of the surcharge on commercial insurance policyholders will likely ultimately be borne by the general public. Second, even when the federal government recoups 100 percent of its initial payout, taxpayers effectively provide an interest-free loan to the target insurers because recoupment occurs in the year(s) after the event. However, the magnitude of these indirect effects would not decrease if the formal taxpayers' share were reduced; in fact, in some cases, the magnitude would increase.

Uninsured Losses Under TRIA

TRIA helps reduce uninsured terrorism losses by making coverage available and by limiting target insurers' exposure. However, our analysis shows that, even with TRIA in place, a high fraction of losses would go uninsured in each of the attack scenarios examined. Uninsured fractions range from 13 percent of the total loss in the indoor anthrax scenario to 57 percent in the outdoor anthrax scenario.

Above we discussed two options for reducing the expected uninsured losses: (1) extending the "make-available" provision of TRIA to include CBRN attack coverage and (2) making terrorism coverage mandatory. Analysis of the former option shows that it would significantly reduce uninsured losses in the two anthrax scenarios, assuming take-up rose from the current 3 percent to 40 percent. As for the latter option, it could sharply reduce or eliminate uninsured losses, but it faces a host of impediments.

Another alternative that would reduce uninsured losses is to decrease insurer deductibles or co-payments. While the Treasury Secretary has stated that "[t]he Administration would accept an extension [of TRIA] only if it . . . increases the dollar deductibles and percentage co-payments" (Snow, 2005), that concern is based on the desire to minimize the government's financial responsibility under TRIA—a concern that is largely unwarranted based on our analysis. In fact, reducing uninsured losses may ultimately reduce taxpayer liability. As demonstrated most recently with Hurricane Katrina, governments often feel compelled to compensate uninsured victims after a disaster. As such, the expectation of post-disaster assistance can actually undermine the demand for insurance against future catastrophes. Thus, facilitating the purchase of insurance may decrease the ultimate taxpayer burden.

Target Insurer Subsidy

A core element of TRIA is its risk-spreading formula that limits the exposure of target insurers in a terrorist attack. After target insurers pay claims, they are partially reimbursed for their losses by funds that ultimately derive from general commercial insurance policyholders and from taxpayers. The fact that primary target insurers' losses are subsidized has been identified as a potentially serious flaw of TRIA. According to some arguments, by subsidizing target insurer losses, TRIA crowds out development of some reinsurance markets, impedes efforts to price premiums accurately and to link premium prices to risk-reduction measures, and delays the development of private capacity to absorb any future losses. In effect, the argument states that the design of TRIA actually undermines its own objective of facilitating the development of a private terrorism insurance market.

While our analysis does not provide any insight into the effect these subsidies may have on the development of a private terrorism insurance market, it does provide quantitative estimates of their magnitude, an important first step toward addressing this issue. We find that, for aircraft impact and indoor anthrax attacks, the subsidy increases from 30 percent of target insurers' loss at a low total loss to 60 percent of target insurers' loss at the TRIA cap of $100 billion in TRIA-covered losses.

At the same time, resolving this issue and ultimately developing a private market will require additional research about the risk of different types of terrorist attacks and about what types of preparedness measures are available to the private sector and how effective they would be. While policyholders could take steps to reduce their risk, options are very limited for some types of attacks, such as an aircraft impact. More generally, however, even if the risk reduction realized from some steps could be quantified, the absolute risk of most terrorist attacks, or even the relative risk in the context of other types of disasters, remains highly uncertain, making premium pricing very difficult.

The Renewal of TRIA

While our analysis is not intended to be a comprehensive analysis of the decision about whether to renew TRIA, our analysis does provide information that bears on the decision. First, to the extent that taxpayer involvement is not a concern for most terrorist attacks, budgetary considerations do not seem relevant as a motivation for allowing TRIA to sunset. We note that TRIA comprises more than a provision for a taxpayer subsidy and hence the lack of a taxpayer role does not mean that TRIA has no influence on the terrorism insurance market. Target insurers still receive substantial subsidies from the surcharge on commercial insurance policyholders, and TRIA makes property insurance for conventional terrorism available to policyholders, both of which act to make terrorism insurance more available and affordable.

Second, since allowing TRIA to sunset will likely increase terrorism insurance premiums and reduce take-up, at least initially, the failure to renew TRIA will likely contribute to the problem of uninsured losses instead of reducing it.

Finally, while one of the arguments against the renewal of TRIA is that the subsidy of target insurer losses discourages efforts to price terrorism insurance and develop a private terrorism insurance market, the relationship between this subsidy and the development of a functional market is quite controversial; as such, determining the validity of the argument will require further study.

Acknowledgments

We gratefully acknowledge extremely helpful formal reviews from Dwight Jaffee at the University of California, Berkeley, and Terry Schell and Melinda Moore at RAND. We also received numerous valuable comments and suggestions throughout the course of this analysis from Howard Kunreuther and his colleagues at the Wharton Risk Management and Decision Process Center, University of Pennsylvania. In addition, we received helpful comments and suggestions from the CTRMP Board and from Robert Reville, Co-director of the CTRMP. We thank Risk Management Solutions both for granting us access to their models and data and for their comments on earlier drafts of this book; Eric Nordman, at the National Association of Insurance Commissioners, for providing data critical to this analysis; and Christina Panis, at RAND, for setting up and running the anthrax release models. Any errors or omissions in the study are the sole responsibility of the authors.

CHAPTER ONE

Introduction

Background

The 9/11 attacks changed the landscape of terrorism loss compensation. Those attacks resulted in at least $20 billion in insured losses (Dixon and Kaganoff-Stern, 2005) and may eventually reach $32 billion in insured losses (Hartwig, 2004). As a result of the substantial losses incurred, insurers questioned their ability to pay claims in future attacks and began to exclude terrorism coverage from commercial insurance policies (U.S. General Accounting Office, 2002; Hubbard and Deal, 2004). In turn, private-sector decisionmakers involved in large real estate developments, building large buildings, and choosing where to locate business operations began to have second thoughts about the advisability, scope, and location of those projects.

The fear that a lack of insurance coverage would threaten economic stability and growth, urban development, and jobs (U.S. General Accounting Office, 2002) led the federal government to adopt the Terrorism Risk Insurance Act (TRIA). TRIA, which is described in more detail in Chapter Two, requires primary commercial property-casualty insurers to offer terrorism insurance coverage. TRIA also includes a risk-spreading scheme that subsidizes the amount that insurers are required to pay in settling claims for terrorist attacks.

The purpose of TRIA is to (1) protect consumers by addressing market disruptions and ensure the continued widespread availability and affordability of property and casualty insurance for terrorism risk and (2) allow for a transitional period for the private markets to stabilize, resume pricing of such insurance, and build capacity to absorb any future losses. Another explicit goal of the TRIA program is to provide an equitable distribution of shared costs of recovery (Bragg, 2005).

TRIA is temporary legislation enacted in November 2002. Unless Congress takes action to extend TRIA, it automatically ceases to be in force at the end of 2005. The pending expiration of TRIA requires that policymakers assess the effectiveness of TRIA and decide whether to extend, modify, or terminate it. This assessment hinges on understanding two related issues: how TRIA will redistribute losses among the different parties under different circumstances and how the assurance of risk spreading will influence decisions that will affect economic stability and growth.

This assessment is complicated by the fact that there have been no large terrorist attacks in the United States since 9/11. Consequently, policymakers have few empirical data on which to base an assessment of the likely effects of TRIA in response to a major terrorist attack. This lack of data makes it difficult to address issues directly related to the distribution of losses, such as the relative shares paid by various parties. The distribution of losses also influences the effectiveness of TRIA in promoting economic stability and growth. How insurers, lenders, developers, and others behave over the long term will likely depend strongly on how losses from large terrorist attacks are expected to be distributed among different parties under TRIA. Because there have been no attacks for which TRIA has been activated, existing evaluations of the effect of TRIA (e.g., U.S. Department of the Treasury, 2005; Congressional Budget Office, 2005; Hubbard and Deal, 2004; Smetters, 2004) may not reflect the ultimate impact of TRIA on affected parties and how those parties' responses would influence the insurance market and overall economic stability and growth.

This study is designed to provide policymakers with empirical estimates of the likely effects of TRIA on the distribution of losses resulting from terrorist attacks. We simulate the expected losses for different terrorist attack scenarios and then examine the effects of the insurance system and TRIA on the ultimate distribution of the losses under different circumstances. These results show how TRIA, as currently written, is likely to respond to the losses that might result from a different attack mode and different loss magnitudes. We then examine the likely effects of changes to each of TRIA's major provisions on the ultimate distribution of losses. This part of the analysis shows which provisions of the act would have to be changed in which ways to produce a desired change in the effects of TRIA. We do not examine the possible responses of private-sector decisionmakers in this study; we leave that question to future work.

Research Approach

The overall study presented in this book consists of three major components. First, we simulate the anticipated losses and the effects of the current insurance system on a number of different scenarios for each of three different modes of terrorist attacks: crashing a hijacked aircraft into a major building, releasing anthrax within a major building, and releasing anthrax outdoors in a major urban area. Second, we estimate the likely effects of TRIA on the ultimate distribution of the losses resulting from each of the individual attack scenarios as well as for cumulative annual losses resulting from the different attack modes examined. Third, we identify the provisions of TRIA that affect the extent to which it redistributes losses among various parties and estimate the effects of changing each of those provisions on TRIA's redistribution function. We compare the effects of TRIA on the loss distribution for different attack modes and for different cumulative annual losses to illustrate the similarities and differences in TRIA's response to different kinds of attacks or to different loss magnitudes. Our analytical approach is summarized in Figure 1.1.

We begin with an event model, which uses physical principles to estimate the effects of a specific type of attack at a specified location. The event model provides estimates of the property damage and casualties that would result from an attack on a specific building or, in the case of an outdoor anthrax attack, a specific metropolitan area somewhere within the United States.

Figure 1.1
Analytical Framework

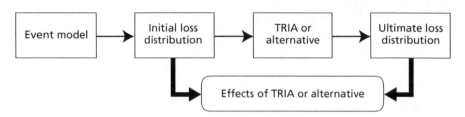

We then estimate the consequent compensation that would be paid to those who initially incurred losses by private insurance under relevant coverages. We apply the estimates of compensation paid by private insurance to the estimates of the losses incurred by various parties as a result of the attack to obtain the initial loss distribution. The initial loss distribution thus describes the distribution of the net losses incurred by various parties as a result of the attack. It includes the net losses incurred by private parties, the initial losses less any compensation paid for those losses from private insurance, and the payments made by private insurers under various coverages.

The TRIA model then estimates how TRIA's risk-sharing provisions would have redistributed losses in each scenario. The application of TRIA to the initial loss distribution gives rise to the ultimate loss distribution; that is, the net losses incurred by various parties after the application of TRIA's risk-sharing provisions.

Finally, we compare the initial loss distribution to the ultimate loss distribution to estimate how TRIA would affect the distribution of losses under different circumstances. This comparison allows us to identify the extent to which TRIA's effects on the distribution of losses vary by attack mode or cumulative annual losses. To estimate the effects of modifications to TRIA, we replace the TRIA model with a modified version of TRIA and compare the ultimate loss distribution under TRIA as currently written to that under TRIA as modified.

Organization of This Book

Chapter Two describes TRIA and its primary risk-sharing provisions. Chapter Three summarizes our analyses of all three types of terrorist attack scenarios and presents our major findings regarding the losses that might be caused by attacks of various modes and sizes. These analyses are detailed in Appendixes A and B. We present our analysis of the effects of TRIA in redistributing the costs of the losses incurred in the various attack scenarios in Chapter Four. Chapter Five presents our analysis of the provisions of TRIA that affect the redistribution of these losses and how changes in these provisions would change the ways in which TRIA would redistribute the losses. Finally, Chapter Six presents some general conclusions of our analysis and their implications for the future of TRIA.

CHAPTER TWO

The Terrorism Risk Insurance Act

Overview

TRIA requires primary insurers to make terrorism coverage available to commercial policyholders. In return for making coverage available, TRIA limits the amount that insurers are responsible for paying by means of a risk-sharing formula. In this formula, a primary insurer is responsible for payouts up to an annual deductible and for a co-payment of 10 percent of all losses above the deductible. Insured losses beyond the deductible and co-payment are paid by a surcharge on all commercial insurance policyholders and by taxpayers.

The requirement to offer coverage and the risk-sharing scheme in TRIA apply to commercial property and casualty policies only; they do not apply to life or health policies or to personal lines such as auto or homeowners' insurance. In addition, TRIA is restricted to certified foreign terrorist attacks only. For an attack to be certified, the perpetrators must have acted on behalf of a foreign person or foreign interest. TRIA does not apply to attacks that are not certified as foreign.

Finally, TRIA allows insurers to exclude property losses from chemical, biological, radiological, and nuclear (CBRN) incidents from policies as long as the exclusion is also applied to losses arising from events other than acts of terrorism. For instance, losses from radiation are routinely excluded from insurance policies and therefore these exclusions apply to terrorism insurance as well. No state allows exclusions on workers' compensation, and therefore terrorism losses are paid under all workers' compensation policies (including CBRN attacks). Losses from a CBRN attack that are insured are eligible for the risk-spreading provision of TRIA.

Figure 2.1 illustrates TRIA's general features. Certain parameters of TRIA have changed from year to year; the figure shows TRIA's 2005 parameters.

The left part of the figure shows the distribution of initial payouts under TRIA. Primary insurers who have paid claims on policies that include terrorism coverage and are in lines covered by TRIA (henceforth "target insurers"[1]) are responsible for payouts up to an annual deductible equal to 15 percent (in 2005) of the insurer's group's annual direct earned premium on TRIA-eligible lines the

Figure 2.1
Summary of Initial and Final Payouts Under TRIA

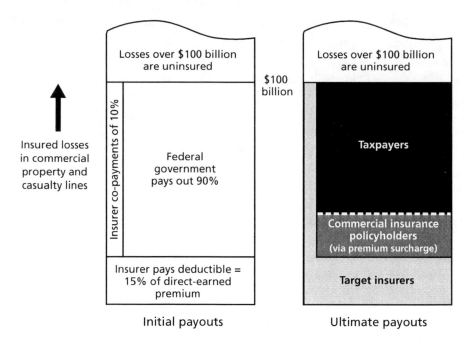

---

[1] We use the term target insurer to refer to insurers with losses on commercial insurance policies covered by TRIA. In practice, many insurers sell commercial insurance as well as other lines (homeowners, auto, life, and health) that are not covered by TRIA.

previous year. A target insurer is also responsible for a co-payment of 10 percent of all losses above the deductible. The remaining 90 percent of losses above the deductible are reimbursed to the insurer by the federal government. This formula is applied for aggregate annual insured losses in TRIA-eligible lines up to $100 billion. TRIA specifies that insurers are not responsible for TRIA-covered losses[2] above $100 billion, but it does not explicitly specify who would be responsible for insured losses in excess of $100 billion.

TRIA also requires that the federal government recoup the difference between an "insurance marketplace aggregate retention amount" ($15 billion in 2005) and the sum of insurer deductibles and co-payments for that year. Recoupment is collected through a surcharge of up to 3 percent per year on all commercial insurance policies in the United States. The right part of Figure 2.1 shows the ultimate distribution of payouts after recoupment.

It is, of course, possible that the government would not attempt to recover these costs following a future terrorist attack. However, the law, as written, requires that the government recoup its payouts. We assume this provision of the law throughout the following analysis.

The initial federal government payout is the difference between the TRIA-covered loss and the sum of the aggregate deductible and the aggregate co-payment. The total amount recouped through the surcharge (S) is given by:

$$S = Min\left(L^{TRIA}, R\right) - \left(D + C\right), \qquad (2.1)$$

where L^{TRIA} = the TRIA-covered loss, R = the insurance marketplace aggregate retention amount, D = the aggregate deductible, and C = the aggregate co-payment. For total annual TRIA-covered losses less than R, S equals the federal payout, and hence the entire federal payout is recouped. If total annual TRIA-covered loss exceeds R, the federal share of losses is only partially recouped, and if the sum of insur-

---

[2] TRIA-covered losses are claims payments made by primary insurers in lines eligible for reimbursement under TRIA.

ers' deductibles and co-payments exceeds R, none of the federal share of losses is recouped.

In addition to the mandatory recoupment amount, TRIA provides the option for additional federal recoupment if economic and other conditions warrant it. It is possible that the government would attempt to recover these costs following a future terrorist attack. However, the law, as written, does not require that the government recoup its payouts in excess of the mandatory recoupment amount. Throughout the following analysis, we assume that the federal government does not seek recoupment of its payouts above the mandatory amount.

Distribution of Losses Under TRIA

As noted above, TRIA is designed to spread the risks of insuring against losses resulting from terrorist attacks. TRIA does not apply to the losses incurred in a terrorist attack that have not been insured. TRIA formally distributes the losses resulting from a terrorist attack among five groups: (1) people and businesses who lack coverage for terrorism losses and must, therefore, bear the losses themselves ("uninsured"), (2) insurers of losses covered by policies in insurance lines not eligible for TRIA coverage such as life and health insurers, (3) primary insurers of losses covered by policies in commercial insurance lines that are eligible for TRIA coverage ("target insurers"), (4) all commercial insurance policyholders in the country, from whom the federal government recoups all or part of its initial payout ("commercial policyholders"), and (5) taxpayers. Five provisions of the law—insurance availability and take-up, TRIA eligibility, deductibles and co-payments, insurance marketplace retention, and the ceiling on insurers' responsibility—determine how the losses resulting from a terrorist attack are redistributed among these five groups. Figure 2.2 illustrates the TRIA provisions that influence the share of terrorist attack losses redistributed to each of these groups.

Figure 2.2
Influence of TRIA Provisions on Loss Distribution

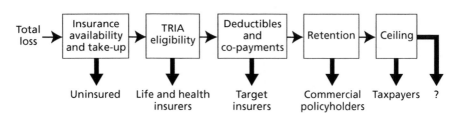

Insurance Availability and Take-Up

TRIA does nothing to spread the losses incurred by those who suffer an injury to their persons or property for which they have not purchased insurance. However, TRIA does influence the take-up of terrorism insurance coverage in two ways: by mandating that insurers offer coverage for certain losses resulting from terrorist attacks and by limiting the amount that insurers are responsible for paying, thereby allowing premiums to be lower than they would be without TRIA. Under TRIA, insurers must offer coverage for property losses from conventional terrorist attacks, although policyholders may decline to purchase that coverage. Insurers may choose to offer property coverage for terrorist CBRN attacks, and policyholders are free to decline the offer if they so choose. In addition, TRIA does not alter the requirement that workers' compensation policies must include coverage for losses from all perils, including terrorist attacks.

The fraction of commercial policyholders who purchase terrorism coverage when it is offered, generally termed the take-up, determines what fraction of the total losses resulting from a terrorist attack will be incurred by policyholders who declined to purchase terrorism coverage ("uninsured").

TRIA Eligibility

TRIA does nothing to spread the losses incurred by a line of insurance that is not eligible for TRIA coverage. As currently written, TRIA is explicitly limited to commercial lines of property and casualty insurance, including excess insurance, workers' compensation, and surety insurance. Specific lines eligible for TRIA are listed in Abernathy (2003). Insurer losses in other insurance lines are not eligible for reimbursement under TRIA. For example, life insurers who had not excluded coverage of deaths caused by terrorist attacks would compensate the survivors of policyholders killed in a terrorist attack. But, TRIA would do nothing to spread the costs that life insurers incurred as a result of the attack. Similarly, TRIA would do nothing to spread the costs that insurers incurred in paying claims for health insurance or personal line policies such as homeowners or automobile insurance. TRIA-eligibility determines which insured losses resulting from a terrorist attack are subject to loss sharing under TRIA.

For most attacks on targets, losses in personal lines will be minimal, and thus noncommercial insurers will be primarily life and health insurers.

Deductibles and Co-Payments

Under TRIA, target insurers compensate policyholders for covered losses incurred in a terrorist attack. The target insurers are then reimbursed by the federal government for claims payments in TRIA-covered lines in excess of their deductible and co-payments. The TRIA deductible and co-payment provisions determine the amount of TRIA-covered losses retained by the target insurers. Deductibles and co-payments are paid by "target insurers."

Aggregate Insurance Marketplace Retention

TRIA requires that the federal government recoup the difference between an insurance marketplace aggregate retention amount ($15 billion in 2005) and the sum of insurer deductibles and co-payments for that year. The specified retention amount determines what part of the losses above the deductible and co-payment is paid by commercial policyholders through the commercial policy surcharge ("commercial policyholders").

Although this share is collected through a policyholder surcharge, because the surcharge effectively increases the cost of commercial insurance in subsequent years, this share will ultimately be paid by policyholders, insurers, and the general public. Presumably, some commercial insurance purchasers are on the margin in the sense that, if the price is increased, they will decline to purchase insurance they would otherwise have bought. In other cases, the insurer will reduce its price for the policy rather than lose the business. Consequently, the surcharge will effectively be partially paid by policyholders who end up paying somewhat more for their policies and partially paid by insurers who lose some business and receive lower prices on some of the business they retain. Ultimately, some of the costs of the surcharges will be passed on to the general public as commercial policyholders pass on some of the increases in their insurance costs to customers in the form of higher prices for the goods and services they sell. The rest of the surcharge costs will be absorbed by employees and shareholders of insurers and commercial businesses that lose business because of the higher costs and make smaller profits on the business they retain. We do not attempt to estimate the ultimate incidence of the policyholder surcharge and treat it as an undivided whole amount in this book.

Coverage Ceiling

TRIA specifies that insurers are not responsible for TRIA-covered losses above $100 billion. The federal government reimburses target insurers for TRIA-covered losses in excess of their deductible and co-payments and recoups the difference, if positive, between the aggregate insurance marketplace retention and the sum of insurer deductibles and co-payments for that year. Thus, taxpayers ultimately pay for TRIA-covered losses above the larger of either the aggregate insurance marketplace retention or the sum of target insurers' deductible and co-payments, up to $100 billion. The law, as currently written, leaves the determination of whether TRIA-covered losses in excess of $100 billion will be paid and, if so, by whom.

The five TRIA provisions highlighted in Figure 2.2 determine how terrorist attack losses will be distributed to each of five groups. Accordingly, any change in one or more of these provisions will affect the ways in which terrorist attack losses will be distributed to each of these groups. And, to achieve a desired change in the ways in which terrorist attack losses will be distributed to each of these groups, one or more of these provisions would have to be modified.

CHAPTER THREE

Terrorist Attack Scenarios

To provide an accurate basis on which to examine the effects of TRIA, we examined in detail the losses that would be expected in three types of large terrorist attacks: an aircraft impact into a tall building, an anthrax release inside a major building, and an outdoor anthrax release in a major urban area. This chapter summarizes the modeling methodology and results. The methodology and results are discussed in detail in Appendix A.

The treatment of terrorist attack losses under TRIA depends on the insurance line under which a given loss is covered. The objective of the modeling, therefore, was to estimate terrorist attack losses and to estimate the extent to which those losses would be covered by different types of insurance. Our general modeling approach entailed selecting an event scenario; modeling the hazard footprint, or the value of damage-causing agents as a function of position; converting the hazard into casualties and property damage; and estimating the compensation paid for those losses by different insurance lines. Much of our modeling utilized the Risk Management Solutions (RMS) Probabilistic Terrorism Model.[1] Some parts of the simulations also utilized models developed by RAND and by federal government agencies (see Appendix A).

---

[1] RMS is a leading provider of models and services for catastrophe risk management. Through the CTRMP, RAND has full access to the RMS terrorism model for use in policy analysis. RAND and RMS worked together closely to ensure that model data, assumptions, and limitations are accurately accounted for in the analysis.

The attack modes selected represent feasible attacks and indeed were chosen because they involve methods (aircraft impact) or materials (anthrax) that have been used in previous terrorist attacks. They also represent a range of potential outcomes and therefore can provide some information on the robustness of TRIA. However, any individual scenario should be regarded as a very low probability event. No attempt is made in this study to estimate probabilities.

Attack Scenarios

Aircraft Impact

Aircraft impacts were simulated with the RMS model and consist of a fully fueled large commercial aircraft impacting a tall building in a major metropolitan area. The model assumes complete collapse of the target building and accounts for damage to neighboring structures. We examined aircraft impact attacks at each of 454 actual buildings in the United States, including every building over 40 stories, plus some smaller, "high profile" buildings that have particularly high visibility or symbolic value. Our analysis focuses on the results for one particular large building, the "major office building," which falls in the 93rd percentile among all buildings analyzed in terms of total casualties. We focus on a scenario near the high end of the range because, as we show below, losses from even very large aircraft impacts are small compared with the loss range for which TRIA applies. Simulations account for the characteristics of the target building; the density and characteristics of the neighboring buildings; the time of occurrence; and the number, occupational status, and age distribution of the occupants. We simulated mid-afternoon, weekday attacks because office buildings are most fully occupied at this time, which would maximize the casualty losses.

The aircraft impact attack, which is similar to the one employed on 9/11, is intended to represent a large-scale conventional (in contrast to CBRN) attack and was selected because of its tragic familiarity. Indeed, inasmuch as TRIA was a response to 9/11, the aircraft impact attack is the type of attack for which TRIA was designed (Chalk et al., 2005).

Indoor Anthrax Release

In the indoor anthrax attack scenario, a sprayer is placed in a room on the ground floor of a large building and aerosolized dry anthrax spores are distributed throughout the building by the building's air circulation system.[2] Our analysis explicitly addressed the effect of filtering in the air circulation system. The time of release is set to 9 a.m. to maximize the number of people exposed and their duration of exposure—anthrax spores can linger indoors for many hours.

We assume that the release occurs undetected and that the attack is discovered three days after release through clinical diagnosis of early victims.[3] Consequently, we assume that the number of exposed people includes those in the building at the time of the release plus a fraction of those who enter the building over the next three days (see Appendixes A and B for details).

This anthrax attack, while unprecedented, is adopted in this study to examine the outcomes of TRIA in a CBRN attack. Anthrax was chosen because of the precedent of the anthrax attacks in September and October of 2001, which showed that such an attack is well within the capability of terrorists (though the 2001 attacks used a less effective method of delivery and caused far fewer casualties than the one studied here).

Outdoor Anthrax Release

In this scenario, a sprayer mounted on a moving truck releases 75 kilograms of anthrax-containing slurry as it drives along a 5-kilometer linear path. The resulting anthrax cloud extends many kilometers

---

[2] The indoor anthrax release was modeled with the CONTAMW Multizone Airflow and Contaminant Transport Model from the National Institute of Standards and Technology (Dols and Walton, 2002).

[3] The material, equipment, and manpower required to execute an attack can easily escape detection at the time of attack. Moreover, the infected victims would take one to six days to show symptoms. We assume that anthrax is suspected through the symptoms of early patients and confirmed by laboratory tests.

downwind of the release path.[4] The attack targets a highly populated, metropolitan area in which the population density is modeled as zones of progressively decreasing density. As in the indoor release case, the release takes place at 9 a.m. in order to catch workers at the beginning of their workday and maximize their duration of exposure.

Most of the casualties would take place inside buildings, as there are typically many more people indoors than outdoors.[5] To determine the indoor dose level, we first calculate the outdoor dose levels at various heights where building air inlets are located then determine the dose reduction factor caused by the buildings to quantify the dose level inside the buildings. The dose reduction inside buildings depends on a building's filtering efficiency, which is greater for downtown office buildings than it is for surrounding suburbs.

Terrorism experts differ widely in their assessments of the difficulty of successfully perpetrating an attack of this magnitude using anthrax. However, it is clear that the country should consider the full spectrum of threats.

Losses and Compensation by Insurance Line

Terrorist attack losses are defined in terms of casualties and property damage. Casualties are classified into six categories: (1) medical only, (2) temporary total disability, (3) permanent partial disability—minor, (4) permanent partial disability—major, (5) permanent total disability, and (6) fatal.[6] Property damage is classified into three categories: building, contents, and business interruption.

Losses in the aircraft impact scenario were estimated with the RMS model and include casualties and property damage in the collapsed target building and neighboring structures, as well as business interruption losses resulting from a civil authority exclusion zone

---

[4] The outdoor anthrax release was modeled with the Chemical/Biological Agent Vapor, Liquid, and Solid Tracking model (Bauer and Gibbs, 2001).

[5] We have assumed that all casualties occur indoors.

[6] These categories correspond to standard definitions used for workers' compensation

around the incident site.[7] Indirect, macroeconomic effects of a ter-rorist attack may be substantial. However, these effects extend beyond the influence of insurance and thus are not germane to a discussion of TRIA. Casualty losses in the anthrax scenarios were estimated with an expanded version of a model developed recently at RAND (Chow et al., n.d.) and include the effects of not only anthrax infection but also antibiotic prophylaxes and medical treatments. This model assigns anthrax casualties to four of the six categories; the model assumes there will be no permanent partial disabilities. Property damage in the anthrax scenarios was estimated with the RMS model and includes building decontamination and business interruption.

For the aircraft impact and the anthrax scenarios, we used the RMS model to estimate how the private-sector insurance system would compensate various parties for the losses they would incur. To simplify our loss calculations, our estimates of insured loss neglect insurance premiums, policyholder deductibles, co-payments, and policy limits. In reality, these costs would be borne by policyholders. By neglecting these factors, we effectively lump the policyholders' share in with the insurers' share and do not include a separate policy-holders' share. Thus, the total loss is not affected, but we overestimate the target insurers' share by an amount equal to what policyholders would be responsible for paying. The magnitude of the policyholders' share, however, is generally expected to be small. Deductibles and co-payments for terrorism coverage are typically the same as for all other perils and so are likely to represent a small fraction of the loss. Ter-rorism premiums are also expected to be a small fraction of the loss.[8] Policy limits, however, may lead to a non-negligible policyholder share. According to Doherty et al. (2005), in many cases, policyhold-ers have not purchased, or have been unable to obtain, insurance for the full value of the property. In such a case, the policyholder would

---

[7] Business interruption losses include only losses from business closure and do not include indirect losses such as decreased sales.

[8] The average premium price for terrorism insurance in 2004 was 0.0057 percent of total insured value (U.S. Department of the Treasury, 2005). The ten-year cumulative premium for an attack resulting in a $5 billion insured loss would be $2.9 million.

be responsible for losses over the limit. For cases where a building is completely destroyed, this may be a significant fraction of the total loss.

We assume that workers injured at their place of work are compensated at the workers' compensation rates in the state in which they were injured. Workers and non-workers are also compensated by various forms of life and health insurance at national average penetration rates and coverage levels. Penetration rates and coverage levels vary by insurance line and type of population. For example, we assume that 60 percent of employed professionals have individual life insurance at an average coverage of $150,000.[9]

In estimating insurance payments for property damage, we assume insurance will cover the full replacement value of insured commercial buildings that are damaged or destroyed in an attack. Compensation levels for contents and business interruption losses are estimated at average insured values.

Tables 3.1 and 3.2 illustrate the estimates we developed for each scenario we ran for each attack mode. Table 3.1 shows the estimated casualty distributions for an aircraft impact into one of the largest office buildings in the country ("Major Office Building" or MOB), an indoor anthrax release in the same major office building, and an outdoor anthrax release.

The outdoor anthrax attack leads to the largest number of casualties, over two million, with over 36,000 deaths. This extreme catastrophic scenario exceeds the size of the other two scenarios by an order of magnitude, and therefore it will illustrate the performance of TRIA in an attack far larger than 9/11. The indoor anthrax attack leads to the smallest number of casualties, though with greater severity: Serious injuries and fatalities both exceed the aircraft impact attack.

---

[9] Coverage rates and levels for some target areas such as New York City likely exceed national averages; thus, the model may underestimate life and health insurance losses in such areas.

Table 3.1
Casualty Distributions for Terrorist Attack Scenarios

Casualty Type	Aircraft Impact (Major Office Building)	Indoor Anthrax (Major Office Building)	Outdoor Anthrax (Major Urban Area)
Medical only	35,524	5,500	1,901,476
Temporary total disability	641	1,500	19,960
Permanent partial disability—minor	561	—	—
Permanent partial disability—major	401	—	—
Permanent total disability	430	4,500	59,881
Fatal	2,632	2,750	36,594
Total	40,188	14,250	2,017,911

Table 3.2
Allocation of Losses by Insurance Line for Terrorist Attack Scenarios
(in millions of dollars)

Insurance Line	Aircraft Impact (Major Office Building)	Indoor Anthrax (Major Office Building)	Outdoor Anthrax (Major Urban Area)
Property	$4,482	$1,061	$100,414
Workers' compensation	$1,522	$6,115	$43,472
Group life	$307	$323	$2,472
Individual life	$235	$247	$2,109
Accidental death and dismemberment	$121	$208	$1,483
Health	$1	$10	$22,354
Total	$6,668	$7,964	$172,304

Table 3.2 shows the insured losses for each of the three scenarios across lines of insurance. Obviously, the outdoor anthrax attack has the largest losses overall, and in every line of insurance as well. The indoor anthrax attack, despite lower casualties, has total losses that are of similar (slightly higher) magnitude as the aircraft impact attack, reflecting the higher severity of injury and therefore higher costs.

The distribution of losses among insurance lines varies across the scenarios. Property losses account for 13 percent of the total loss in the indoor anthrax scenario, 58 percent of the total in the outdoor anthrax scenario, and 67 percent of the total in the aircraft impact scenario. Workers' compensation shows a complementary variation, accounting for 77 percent of the losses in indoor anthrax, 25 percent in outdoor anthrax, and 23 percent in the aircraft impact. Life and health lines[10] make up 10 percent in the indoor anthrax and aircraft impact scenarios and 16 percent in the outdoor anthrax scenario. A comparison between the aircraft impact simulation and the actual losses from the World Trade Center (WTC) attacks on 9/11 is given in Appendix A.

As discussed in Appendix A, there is great uncertainty about any eventual liability losses from 9/11, so we omit potential liability losses from this analysis. Briefly, after 9/11, Congress limited the liability of most defendants and created the 9/11 Victims' Compensation Fund, which significantly lowered the ultimate liability losses. It is unclear whether this will occur in future attacks. If liability is not limited in future attacks, we would expect that the financial losses could be significantly higher than the estimates reported here.

The allocation of losses by insurance line listed in Table 3.2 forms the basis for our analysis of the effects of TRIA on the ultimate distribution of losses after a large terrorist attack.

---

[10] We define life and health insurer losses as the sum of losses from group life, individual life, accidental death and dismemberment, and health lines.

CHAPTER FOUR

The Distribution of Terrorist Attack Losses Under TRIA

We estimated how terrorism losses would be distributed among various parties under TRIA. Our analysis is based on the losses and allocation of losses by insurance line estimated for the attack scenarios described in Chapter Three. Calculating how losses would be distributed under TRIA requires estimating the fraction of the total loss that is insured and the fraction of insured loss that is eligible for TRIA. TRIA-covered losses are then apportioned to various parties according to the loss-sharing scheme defined in TRIA.

Uninsured Loss

The uninsured loss from a terrorist attack is simply the difference between the total loss and the insured loss. In the context of TRIA, the insured losses consist of those losses not eligible for TRIA, which comprise life and health losses in this analysis, and TRIA-covered losses, which comprise commercial property and workers' compensation losses. The following sections discuss how each of these loss types is estimated.

Life and Health Insurer Loss

Losses to life and health insurers are not eligible for TRIA. In this analysis, we define life and health insurer losses as the sum of losses in group life, individual life, accidental death and dismemberment, and health lines. Life and health insurer losses for the three scenarios we examined are given in Table 3.2.

TRIA-Covered Loss

The TRIA-covered loss is the part of the total loss eligible for reimbursement under TRIA and comprises workers' compensation and insured commercial property losses. In an attack on a major building, the TRIA-covered loss, L_i^{TRIA}, is:

$$L_i^{TRIA} = L_i^{total} \frac{TL_{MOB}^{prop} + L_{MOB}^{WC}}{L_{MOB}^{total}}, \quad (4.1)$$

where L_i^{total} is the total loss, T is the fraction of property loss that is insured against terrorism (insurance take-up) and L_{MOB}^{prop}, L_{MOB}^{WC}, and L_{MOB}^{total} are the modeled property, workers' compensation, and total losses, respectively, for the aircraft impact or indoor anthrax release in the major office building scenario.[1] T is applied to the property loss only because workers' compensation coverage is mandatory and terrorism coverage cannot be excluded.

For the outdoor anthrax attack in a major urban area (MUA), the TRIA-covered loss is given by:

$$L_i^{TRIA} = L_i^{total} \frac{TL_{MUA}^{prop} + L_{MUA}^{WC}}{L_{MUA}^{total}}, \quad (4.2)$$

---

[1] Estimating the TRIA-covered fraction of total loss using the WTC losses from Hartwig (2004) gives a value very similar (within 5 percent) to the value we get using the MOB simulation results.

where L_{MUA}^{prop}, L_{MUA}^{WC}, and L_{MUA}^{total} are the property, workers' compensation, and total losses (shown in Table 3.2), respectively, for the modeled outdoor anthrax release in a major urban area.

Note that losses from life and health lines are not eligible for TRIA coverage and are not included in Equations (4.1) or (4.2).

Target Insurer Loss

The target insurer loss is the target insurers' share of the TRIA-covered losses, which consists of deductibles and co-payments made by primary insurers in lines eligible for reimbursement under TRIA. Our method for estimating deductibles and co-payments is explained below.

Aggregate Insurance Industry Annual TRIA Deductible

Under TRIA, each target insurer compensates its policyholders for covered losses incurred in a terrorist attack. Commercial target insurers are then reimbursed by the federal government for payments in TRIA-covered lines in excess of their annual deductible and co-payments. Because each target insurer's deductible depends on its group's direct-earned premiums, each target insurer faces a unique deductible. Our concern is how TRIA affects the distribution of losses among different types of parties; we do not attempt to predict how individual insurers will fare in a terrorist attack. Accordingly, we compute an aggregate deductible for multiple insurers based on estimates of average insurer characteristics and do not attempt to estimate deductibles for each individual insurer.

To estimate the total losses paid by target insurers under TRIA, we must first estimate the aggregate insurance industry annual deductible specified by TRIA for the insurers involved in the attack (aggregate deductible). However, because of the way insurer deductibles are calculated under TRIA, the aggregate deductible is difficult to predict. Unlike more familiar deductibles used in insurance policies, insurer deductibles under TRIA are not defined in terms of losses. An individual target insurer's deductible is based on its group's premium, so the aggregate deductible depends on the number and size of insurance companies incurring TRIA-covered losses. Because there is no way to predict which insurers will incur terrorism losses over the course of a year, there is no direct way to estimate the aggregate deductible.

Thus, a significant challenge in estimating the allocation of losses under TRIA is uncertainty in the number of insurers affected by a given attack. A simple analysis might assume that a single insurer is involved. While there may be some situations where this is the case (such as an attack on a corporate headquarters building where the corporation is the sole occupant of the building and where a single insurer writes all the insurance for the target corporation), this is typically not the case. Because multiple insurers are affected by the attack, the calculation of the distribution among insurers, policyholders, and taxpayers will change.

We use data on the identities and losses of the insurers involved in the World Trade Center attack to develop a series of assumptions about the aggregate deductible that would apply in a terrorist attack on a building and its immediate neighbors. We use these assumptions to estimate what the aggregate effective deductible would be in a terrorist attack on a building and then use those estimates to explore the effects of TRIA in response to aircraft impact and indoor anthrax attack scenarios. Because we have no reason to believe the available data provide a basis for estimating the deductibles that would apply in an outdoor anthrax attack, we employ an entirely different series of assumptions to explore the effects of TRIA in response to an outdoor anthrax attack scenario.

Deductible for Aircraft Impact and Indoor Anthrax Attacks. The vast majority of the damage in the aircraft impact and indoor anthrax attack scenarios is inflicted on the target building and its immediate neighbors. Consequently, the vast majority of losses are incurred by insurers on the target building and the tenants in that building. While there is no way of knowing which targets will be attacked in the future, our limited experience indicates that terrorists are likely to target large, high-profile buildings in major metropolitan areas for both aircraft impact and indoor anthrax attacks. If this pattern continues for future attacks, it may be reasonable to assume that a similar cross-section of insurers will be affected by aircraft impact and indoor anthrax attacks. Based on this assumption, we estimate the TRIA deductible for these scenarios in the same way.

Because data on identities of the insurers involved at any particular site are not generally available, we have made several assumptions to estimate what the aggregate insurance industry deductible would be in any particular scenario that involves an attack on a building.

To begin, we assume that the number of primary insurers involved in any particular site is proportional to net insured loss. This assumption reflects three subsidiary assumptions. First, we assume that at any potential target, any one insurer is willing to accept up to a certain amount of exposure but not more than that amount of exposure. Second, we assume that insurers are able to accurately assess risk. These two assumptions imply that the number of primary insurers involved in a target is proportional to the risk. The third subsidiary assumption is that the losses resulting from a terrorist attack on any site are proportional to the insured risk for that site. Taken together, these assumptions imply that the loss incurred at a site reflects the risk, which, in turn, reflects the number of insurers involved at that site.

Our next main assumption is that the distribution of insurer sizes as measured by direct-earned premiums on TRIA-eligible lines at any potential target site is, on average, the same as it was for the WTC in September 2001.

Finally, because many insurers' losses will be less than their formal deductibles, the effective aggregate deductible will be less than the sum of the formal deductibles of all target insurers involved. We account for this by assuming that in any future attack, the fraction of the total insured losses surpassing deductibles will be the same as would have been the case for the WTC attacks if TRIA had been in place then. That is, the proportion of total target insurers' losses that will exceed the sum of their individual deductibles in any future attack will be about the same, on average, as the corresponding proportion that would have been experienced at the WTC. This is a reasonable corollary of our first assumption that the number of insurers (and hence aggregate deductible) scales with total insured loss. Given this assumption, the effective deductible is a constant fraction of the formal deductible.

Under these assumptions, the aggregate deductible for the target insurers involved in any attack, i, is equal to the TRIA-covered loss for that attack normalized to the aggregate deductible/loss for the World Trade Center:

$$D_i = L_i^{TRIA} \, D_{WTC}^{eff} \big/ L_{WTC}^{TRIA} \, , \tag{4.3}$$

where D_i is the aggregate deductible, L_i^{TRIA} is the TRIA-covered loss given by equation 4.1, and $D_{WTC}^{eff} \big/ L_{WTC}^{TRIA}$ is the ratio of aggregate deductible to TRIA-covered loss for the World Trade Center (see Appendix C).

Deductible for Outdoor Anthrax Attack. In contrast to the aircraft impact and indoor anthrax attack scenarios, in which most of the damage is inflicted on a single building, damage in an outdoor anthrax release will be dispersed over hundreds of square kilometers. Under these circumstances, it is likely that far more insurers will incur losses than did in the World Trade Center attacks. In terms of direct-earned premiums, insurers incurring losses in the World Trade Center attacks represented over 35 percent of the nation's total commercial property/casualty insurance. Given that such a significant fraction of insurance capacity was involved in an incident, albeit large, that included a small number of insured sites, we assume that an outdoor anthrax attack affecting hundreds or thousands of insured sites in a major metropolitan area will involve the vast majority of commercial property/casualty insurers in the country. We further assume that, with so many insurers involved, individual insurers' losses will be less than their TRIA deductible as long as the total loss is less than the maximum national aggregate deductible. The aggregate deductible cannot exceed the sum of individual insurers' deductibles. Based on National Association of Insurance Commissioners (NAIC) data, this maximum aggregate deductible is approximately $44 bil-lion.[2] For events with losses greater than $44 billion, we assume that all insurers reach their deductible simultaneously.

Under these assumptions, the aggregate deductible is simply equal to the smaller of the TRIA-covered loss or $44 billion:

$$D_i = L_i^{TRIA}, \text{ for } L_i^{TRIA} \leq \$44 \text{ billion}, \tag{4.4a}$$

$$D_i = \$44 \text{ billion, for } L_i^{TRIA} > \$44 \text{ billion}, \tag{4.4b}$$

where L_i^{TRIA} is given by Equation (4.2).

Aggregate Insurer Co-Payment

The target insurer co-payment under TRIA is equal to 10 percent of all TRIA-covered losses above the insurer deductible. In terms of the aggregate deductible, the aggregate insurer co-payment (C_i) is given by:

$$C_i = 0.1\left(L_i^{TRIA} - D_i\right). \tag{4.5}$$

Distribution of Losses Under TRIA

The relationships given by Equations (4.1) through (4.5) allow us to compute the distribution of terrorism losses among the various parties under TRIA. We first examine the TRIA loss distributions for the specific scenarios modeled in Chapter Three and then explore more generally how TRIA loss distributions vary with cumulative annual loss for the three different types of terrorist attacks considered.

---

[2] The sum of the annual direct-earned premium in TRIA-eligible lines for all companies in 2003 was $294 billion; a deductible equal to 15 percent of this sum is $44 billion (Eric Nordman, personal communication with the authors, 2005).

TRIA Loss Distributions for the Three Scenarios

Distributions for the aircraft impact, indoor anthrax, and outdoor anthrax attack scenarios simulated in Chapter Three are shown in Figure 4.1. Values for terrorism insurance take-up came from a survey of commercial property/casualty insurers (U.S. Department of the Treasury, 2005). For non-CBRN coverage, the take-up in 2004 was 54 percent. We use this value for building, contents, and business interruption insurance in the aircraft impact scenario; we assume 100 percent take-up on aircraft hull terrorism insurance. Note that any individual target building in an aircraft impact attack is likely to be either insured or not, so the building coverage take-up in any individual event will be 0 or 1. In using the national average take-up of 54 percent for building coverage we are showing the loss distribution that would be expected for a sample of many events. The take-up of CBRN coverage is less than 3 percent, so we use a 3 percent take-up for the indoor and outdoor anthrax attacks. As discussed above, take-up for workers' compensation coverage in all cases is 100 percent. Take-up values are listed in Table 4.1.

Figure 4.1 shows that substantial portions of the loss would go uninsured in all scenarios. Despite the low CBRN take-up, the fraction of loss that would be uninsured in the indoor anthrax scenario (13 percent) is smaller than that in the aircraft impact scenario (30 percent). This occurs because the majority of losses in the indoor anthrax scenario come from workers' compensation (see Table 4.1), which is 100 percent covered, resulting in a high overall take-up for the indoor anthrax case. The outdoor anthrax scenario would have a much higher proportion of property losses, and hence the low take-up for these lines would result in a high fraction of the loss going uninsured (57 percent).

Life and health insurer losses range from 10 percent in the aircraft impact and indoor anthrax scenarios to 16 percent in the outdoor anthrax scenario. Life and health insurer losses are not eligible for TRIA and hence are the responsibility of the insurer.

Figure 4.1
Distribution of Losses Under TRIA for the Three Attack Scenarios

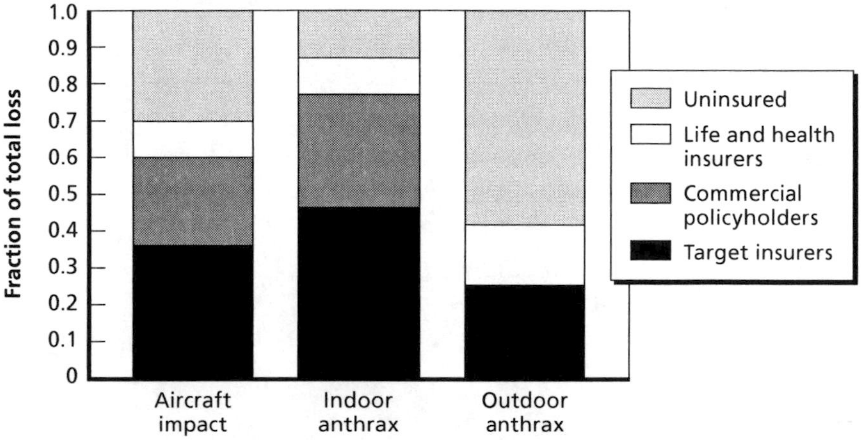

NOTE: Target insurers' share = deductible + co-payment, where deductible is calculated with Equation (4.3) (for aircraft impact and indoor anthrax) or Equations (4.4a) and (4.4b) (outdoor anthrax) and co-payment is given by Equation (4.5); commercial policyholders' share is given by Equation (2.1); life and health insurer share, $L_i^{L\&H}$, is from Table 3.2; and uninsured loss = $L_i^{total} - L_i^{TRIA} - L_i^{L\&H}$.

Table 4.1
Terrorism Coverage Take-Up

	Aircraft Impact		Indoor Anthrax		Outdoor Anthrax	
	Loss Fraction	Take-up	Loss Fraction	Take-Up	Loss Fraction	Take-Up
Property	0.65	0.54	0.13	0.03	0.58	0.03
Aircraft hull	0.02	1.00	—	—	—	—
Workers' compensation	0.23	1.00	0.77	1.00	0.25	1.00
Life and health	0.10	0	0.10	0	0.16	0
Overall	1.00	0.60	1.00	0.77	1.00	0.27

Insured property and workers' compensation losses qualify for the risk-spreading provisions of TRIA. As discussed in Chapter Two, losses above the aggregate insurer deductible and co-payment are paid by the federal government, which may then recoup a portion of that payout by levying a surcharge on all commercial property/casualty insurance policies. In the case of the aircraft impact and indoor anthrax scenarios, the federal government would recoup all of its payout from surcharges on commercial policyholders. In the outdoor anthrax scenario, there is no federal payout and, hence, no recoupment and no commercial policyholder surcharge. TRIA-covered losses in this scenario are less than the industry-wide maximum deductible of $44 billion and so would be paid entirely through the target insurer aggregate deductible.

Our most significant finding is that taxpayers would ultimately pay nothing in any of the scenarios examined. In the aircraft impact and indoor anthrax scenarios, taxpayers would pay nothing because the total loss ($6 billion–$8 billion) would be less than the $15 billion insurance marketplace retention amount specified by TRIA for 2005.[3] For TRIA-covered losses below this retention amount, the federal government recoups all of its initial payout through the commercial policyholder surcharge.

In the outdoor anthrax scenario, taxpayers would pay nothing because of both the low take-up and our assumption that the loss would be shared among a large number of insurers. The low overall take-up for outdoor anthrax means that the insured loss is a small fraction of the total loss, and so the point at which taxpayers begin to subsidize target insurers is displaced to higher total loss. Sharing the loss among many target insurers shifts the point at which the loss exceeds the aggregate deductible to higher total loss. Since federal payouts begin only when the loss exceeds the deductible, this similarly displaces the point at which taxpayers begin to subsidize target insurers to higher total loss.

---

[3] Although the federal government ultimately recoups all its payout so that taxpayers pay nothing directly, this money is recouped from commercial insurance policyholders, which could be considered an indirect tax that affects most citizens. See Chapter Two for more discussion of this point.

TRIA Loss Distributions for Cumulative Annual Losses

We can also use our approach to model the loss distribution under TRIA for cumulative annual losses resulting from multiple events. Target insurers' deductibles and co-payments under TRIA are applied to annual losses. If an insurer suffers losses from multiple events in a single year, these losses are combined to determine when the TRIA deductible has been met. Equations (4.1) and (4.2) are generally applicable to any size cumulative annual loss as long as the relative proportions of workers' compensation and property losses do not vary substantially among the individual attacks entailed in the cumulative annual loss. This condition is well-satisfied for the largest 50 percent of the 454 aircraft impacts we simulated, for which the relative proportions of workers' compensation and property losses are very similar to those for the major office building attack shown in Table 3.2 (see Appendix A). We assume that this condition also holds for anthrax attacks, in which the number of infections (resulting in workers' compensation losses) and the amount of decontamination (resulting in property losses) are expected to scale in proportion to total loss.

Equations (4.4) and (4.5) are also generally applicable to any size cumulative annual loss.

As written, Equation (4.3) allows the aggregate deductible (D) to increase unbounded as L increases. This is equivalent to assuming that each increment of additional loss is incurred by a unique insurer. This is unrealistic for two reasons. First, the aggregate deductible cannot exceed the maximum national aggregate deductible of $44 billion. A second, more restrictive, constraint is that some insurers will have written coverage on multiple attack targets. Once an insurer pays its deductible, any additional loss incurred by that insurer in subsequent events will not have any associated deductible. In this case, D will not rise as quickly as L does, as indicated by Equation (4.3).

We account for the influence of overlapping insurers among targets by estimating the fraction of loss in any event that is covered by insurers that have suffered no loss in prior events (undeducted loss). As the number of events increases, the probability of new insurers being involved decreases, so the incremental addition to the undeducted loss decreases with increasing cumulative loss. The aggregate deductible for any cumulative loss made up of multiple events is determined from the undeducted loss by scaling to the World Trade Center results (see Appendix C for further details):

$$D = \sum_{n=1}^{j} \left(D_{WTC}^{eff} / L_{WTC}^{TRIA} \right) L_{n,total}^{TRIA} \left(1 - \frac{\left(D_{WTC}^{eff} / L_{WTC}^{TRIA} \right) L_{n,total}^{TRIA}}{0.15 P_{total}^{TRIA}} \right)^{n-1} , \quad (4.6)$$

where j is the number of events that generate the cumulative loss, and $L_{n,total}^{TRIA}$ is given by Equation (4.1).

The aggregate deductible given by Equation (4.6) is shown in Figure 4.2 as a function of the cumulative TRIA-covered loss. As the number of events increases, the undeducted loss per event decreases. As a result, as cumulative loss increases, the terms in the summation in Equation (4.6) approach zero, and D approaches the $0.15 P_{total}^{TRIA}$, which is the maximum national aggregate deductible of $44 billion. Figure 4.2 also shows that Equation (4.6) gives effectively indistinguishable values of D for individual loss increments ($L_{n,total}^{TRIA}$), ranging from $1 billion to $5 billion (values of D differ by less than 3 percent).

The actual aggregate deductible in any individual event or for any cumulative annual loss may differ from that predicted by Equation (4.6). As discussed above, office buildings owned by companies that use the entire building for their own employees could conceivably use a single insurance company for the building, contents, business interruption, and workers' compensation coverage. In this case, there would be only one insurer incurring losses in an attack, and the deductible would be lower than that given by Equation (4.6). On the other hand, buildings could house a very large number of different tenants, all of whom could use separate insurers for different insurance lines, such that the aggregate deductible could be greater than

Figure 4.2
Aggregate Deductible Given by Equation (4.6)

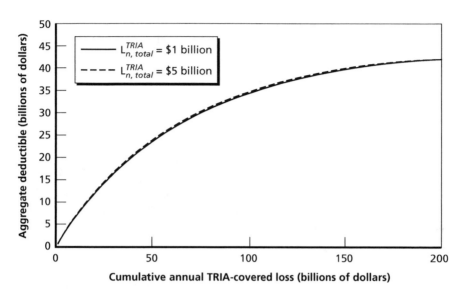

that given by Equation (4.6). Similarly, as pointed out by Doherty et al. (2005), workers' compensation insurance in some states is dominated by a single very large insurer. In such cases, the number of workers' compensation insurers incurring losses will be less than in states with a more competitive workers' compensation market. However, the direct-earned premium, and hence TRIA deductible, of such large insurers will be commensurately large, so that the industry aggregate deductible for a given loss would be similar to that for a situation in which the loss was shared among several smaller insurers. Thus, while the distribution of number and sizes of insurers may vary in different locations, our general assumption that the size of the TRIA aggregate deductible is proportional to the loss remains valid.

Therefore, for cumulative annual losses resulting from multiple terrorist attacks on a variety of different buildings, Equation (4.6) gives a reasonable representation of the expected aggregate deductible.

Loss Distributions for Aircraft Impact and Indoor Anthrax Attacks. Given the aggregate deductible, we can compute the TRIA loss distribution as a function of loss for any of the attack types examined.

Figure 4.3 shows the loss distribution for aircraft impact and indoor anthrax attacks as a function of cumulative annual loss. In each case the maximum cumulative annual loss value shown corresponds to a TRIA-covered loss of $100 billion, which is the TRIA program cap. Each curve in Figure 4.3 shows the portion of the cumulative annual loss that would be paid by various stakeholders, assuming current take-up values.

The results for uninsured and life and health insurer losses are analogous to those for the individual attacks—they represent a constant fraction of the cumulative annual loss. The uninsured losses would be substantial—for a cumulative annual loss of $50 billion, $15 billion would go uninsured if that loss was from aircraft impact attacks and almost $7 billion would go uninsured if the loss was from indoor anthrax attacks. These losses would be the responsibility of building and business owners who had not purchased terrorism insurance.

Up to a cumulative annual loss of approximately $75 billion to $95 billion, the largest share of losses would be paid by the target insurers of the attack sites through the aggregate deductible and co-payment. For a $50 billion loss, target insurers would pay $17.3 billion for aircraft impact attacks and $21.1 billion for indoor anthrax attacks.

TRIA-covered losses beyond the insurer aggregate deductible and co-payment are shared between commercial policyholders and taxpayers. These losses are initially paid by the federal government, which then recoups all or part of its payment with a surcharge on commercial property/casualty insurance policies. The amount recouped in a year is governed by the $15 billion insurance marketplace aggregate retention. The retention limits the total amount that the government can recoup via a surcharge on commercial insurance policyholders.[4] Any part of the initial federal payout that is not re-

---

[4] While the term "insurance marketplace aggregate retention amount" used in TRIA implies a limit on the entire insurance marketplace, there is no limit on the deductible or co-payment amounts.

Figure 4.3
Generalized TRIA Loss Distribution for Cumulative Annual Losses Resulting from Multiple Aircraft Impact and Indoor Anthrax Attacks

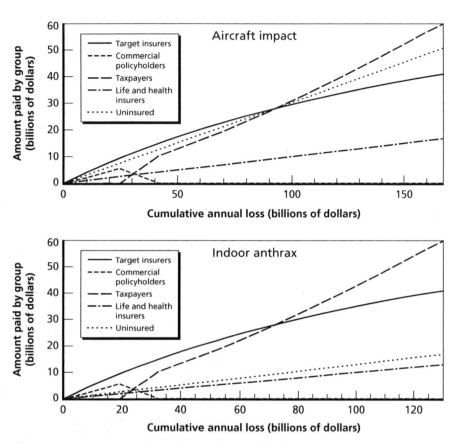

NOTE: Shares are calculated as explained in the note to Figure 4.1, except that the deductible (D) is calculated with Equation (4.6) and the taxpayers' share = $L_i^{TRIA} - (D + C + S)$.

couped is ultimately paid by taxpayers. The result is that the subsidy to target insurers shifts from commercial policyholders to taxpayers as the total loss increases.

The relationship between retention and surcharge is given by Equation (2.1). As losses increase, the commercial policyholders' share increases until the TRIA-covered loss reaches the $15 billion retention amount. For losses above $15 billion, the commercial poli-cyholders' share begins to decrease as the target insurers' deductible and co-payment continue to increase. When the deductible plus co-payment alone reach $15 billion, the commercial policyholders' share drops to zero.[5] In a situation in which the total loss is covered entirely by the aggregate deductible, there would be no federal payout, and hence no recoupment surcharge.

When the recoupment amount begins to decrease, the govern-ment is no longer recouping all of its payout, and taxpayers therefore begin contributing. As noted above, this occurs at a TRIA-covered loss of $15 billion. At the current take-up of terrorism insurance, this corresponds to a total loss at which taxpayers begin to contribute $25 billion for aircraft impact attacks and $20 billion for indoor anthrax attacks. For comparison, the TRIA-covered loss from the World Trade Center attacks would have been approximately $13 billion at current take-up,[6] so taxpayers would not contribute if a similar-sized event occurred today. Our modeling indicates that the loss from a single indoor anthrax attack would be similar to that from an aircraft impact attack (Table 3.2). This makes it clear that there would need to be a minimum of three to four very large aircraft impact or indoor anthrax events in a year before taxpayers would pay part of the loss.

The loss distribution for aircraft impacts in Figure 4.3 is qualita-tively similar to that presented by Doherty et al. (2005) for large truck bombs. The primary differences are that Doherty et al. show no losses in life and health lines and find a higher share for target insur-ers and a lower share for commercial policyholders. Much of the dif-ference in the distribution between target insurers and commercial policyholders stems from the fact that truck bombs are expected to have a greater ratio of workers' compensation to property losses than

---

[5] The federal government is permitted, though not required, to recoup its payouts beyond the minimum amount, in which case the commercial policyholders' share would reach zero at a higher total loss than shown in Figure 4.3.

[6] Estimate based on 100 percent of $2.3 billion in workers' compensation and aviation hull loss plus 54 percent (the current terrorism insurance take-up) of $19.8 billion in other insur-ance lines exclusive of life and health and possible liability losses (loss estimates from Hart-wig, 2004).

that for aircraft impacts. A greater proportion of workers' compensation leads to higher overall take-up, which, in turn, leads to a higher share for target insurers.

Loss Distribution for Outdoor Anthrax Attacks. The loss distribution for outdoor anthrax releases is very different from those for aircraft impacts or indoor anthrax releases. This loss distribution is shown in Figure 4.4, where, as in Figure 4.3, the maximum cumulative annual loss value shown corresponds to a TRIA-covered loss of $100 billion.

For an outdoor anthrax attack, a much higher fraction of losses would be uninsured—out of $50 billion nearly $30 billion would go uninsured at current take-up. The uninsured fraction is much higher than in the indoor anthrax case because of the much lower proportion of workers' compensation losses in an outdoor attack. While the take-up on non–workers' compensation lines is just 3 percent in both cases, workers' compensation losses, for which the take-up is 100 percent, make up 77 percent of the losses in the indoor anthrax case and only 25 percent in the outdoor anthrax case (see Table 4.1).

Figure 4.4
Generalized TRIA Loss Distribution for Cumulative Annual Losses Resulting from Outdoor Anthrax Attacks

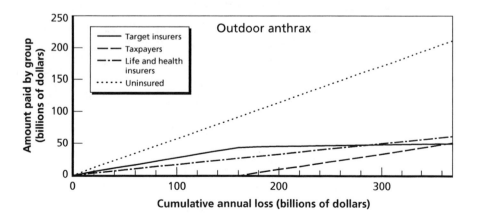

Because we assume that the losses in an outdoor anthrax attack are shared among the vast majority of property/casualty insurers, all TRIA-covered losses up to the industry-wide maximum deductible of $44 billion are paid by target insurers of the attack sites through the aggregate deductible; there would be no surcharge and so general commercial policyholders do not contribute to the losses. The low take-up for CBRN coverage combined with the relatively low proportion of workers' compensation losses expected in an outdoor anthrax attack (25 percent) means that the TRIA-covered loss is much lower than the total loss. At current take-up, the TRIA-covered loss would not reach $44 billion until a total loss of $164 billion (marked by the inflection in the target insurers' share in Figure 4.4). TRIA-covered losses above $44 billion would be paid by the co-payment and taxpayers.

The combination of low overall insurance coverage and distribution of losses among many insurers leads to a situation in which none of the risk-sharing provisions under TRIA would apply to outdoor anthrax attacks until total annual losses exceeded $164 billion. The entire loss up to $164 billion would be the responsibility of insurers and uninsured business owners.

TRIA Loss Distribution Regimes

The results shown in Figures 4.2 and 4.3 illustrate that TRIA creates multiple regimes that differ in terms of the parties' relative shares of terrorism losses. These regimes are summarized in Table 4.2.

Uninsured building and business owners and life and health insurers pay part of any loss and so contribute over the entire loss interval.

TRIA does not take effect until the TRIA-covered losses reach $5 million, so insurers on sites incurring losses (target insurers) pay the entire loss up to this point. Assuming current terrorism insurance take-up, we estimate that TRIA-covered losses will reach $5 million when total losses in aircraft impact attacks reach $8.5 million or total losses in indoor anthrax attacks reach $6.5 million.

Table 4.2
TRIA Loss Distribution Regimes

Who Pays		Total Loss Interval (at current take-up)		
		Aircraft Impact	Indoor Anthrax	Outdoor Anthrax
Uninsured + life and health	Target	$0–$8.5M	$0–$6.5M	$0–$164B
	Target + commercial	$8.5M–$25B	$6.5M–$20B	—
	Target + commercial + taxpayer	$25B–$43B	$20B–$33B	—
	Target + taxpayer	$43B–$167B	$33B–$130B	$164B–$370B
	Unspecified	>$167B	>$130B	>$370B

NOTES: Uninsured = people and businesses who lack coverage for terrorism losses; life and health = insurers of losses in life and health lines, which are not eligible for TRIA coverage; target = insurers of losses covered by policies in commercial insurance lines eligible for TRIA coverage; commercial = all commercial policyholders in the country. M = millions. B = billions.

When total losses exceed these respective values, commercial policyholders begin contributing. Commercial policyholders do not contribute in the outdoor anthrax case and target insurers pay the entire loss up to $164 billion.

In the aircraft impact and indoor anthrax cases, taxpayers begin to contribute once the $15 billion insurance marketplace aggregate retention amount is reached. We estimate that, on average, this would occur at a total loss of about $25 billion ($20 billion) for aircraft impact (indoor anthrax) attacks.

Commercial policyholders cease to contribute once the aggregate deductible plus co-payment reach the $15 billion retention. We estimate that, on average, deductibles and co-payments would reach the retention at a total loss of about $43 billion ($33 billion) for aircraft impact (indoor anthrax) attacks.

Finally, the responsibility for payment of TRIA-covered losses above $100 billion is unspecified. This corresponds to total losses of

$167 billion ($130 billion) for aircraft impact (indoor anthrax) attacks and $370 billion for outdoor anthrax attacks.

CHAPTER FIVE

Distribution of Losses Under Possible Modifications to TRIA

Some observers might object to one or another aspect of the distributions accomplished by TRIA, believing that some group could be allocated an inappropriate share under certain circumstances, such as particular modes or sizes of terrorist attacks. Others might believe that the distributions accomplished by the current TRIA might fail to achieve TRIA's objective of maintaining a viable terrorism insurance market. In either case, TRIA would have to be modified to change the loss distribution. Accordingly, to achieve a desired change in the ways in which terrorist attack losses will be distributed among these groups, TRIA would have to be modified. To help elucidate the effects of various possible modifications to TRIA on the overall loss distribution, we have estimated the loss distribution that would result when the different provisions of TRIA are changed. In each case, we begin with a loss distribution goal and then examine the effect of some possible modifications to TRIA in achieving this goal.

Reduce Uninsured Losses

Uninsured property owners and businesses stand a high probability of financial failure after a large terrorist attack. As also discussed in Chalk et al. (2005), reducing the uninsured losses from terrorism thus has the general benefit of reducing local and national economic repercussions from a terrorist attack. In all of the scenarios above, uninsured losses are significant, and thus policymakers may want to reduce these losses in order to reduce the cascading economic consequences of terrorist attacks.

An additional motivation for reducing uninsured losses can ultimately be to reduce taxpayer liability. In the aftermath of disasters, terrorist or otherwise, governments often feel compelled to compensate uninsured victims. This will undermine the demand for insurance against future catastrophes. This is referred to by economists as the "Samaritan's Dilemma." By appropriately encouraging the purchase of insurance, it may be that the ultimate expected taxpayer burden is lower.

By design, TRIA helps reduce uninsured terrorism losses in two ways: by mandating that insurers offer coverage for certain losses resulting from terrorist attacks and by limiting the amount that insurers are responsible for paying, thereby allowing premiums to be lower than they would be without TRIA. Two possible modifications that may help further reduce the uninsured losses in a terrorist attack are extending the "make-available" requirement for terrorism insurance to include CBRN coverage and making terrorism insurance coverage mandatory in commercial insurance policies.

Mandate CBRN Coverage Availability

TRIA allows insurers to exclude losses from CBRN incidents from policies as long as such policy exclusion is also applied to losses arising from events other than acts of terrorism and it is permitted by applicable state law. Only 35 percent of insurers in TRIA-eligible lines offered CBRN coverage in some of their policies written in 2003 and 2004,[1] and CBRN take-up among policyholders is less than 3 percent (U.S. Department of the Treasury, 2005). Mandating that CBRN coverage be made available to all policyholders could increase take-up and reduce uninsured losses in the event of such an attack.

It is difficult to estimate what the take-up would be if CBRN coverage were universally available. The current low take-up of

---

[1] This estimate represents an upper limit on overall CBRN coverage availability because it could include instances of insurers offering CBRN coverage to only a small fraction of clients.

CBRN insurance stems not only from limited availability, but also a perception among policyholders that they are not at risk (U.S. Department of the Treasury, 2005). Accordingly, we assume that if CBRN coverage were available to all policyholders, take-up would be lower than the 54 percent take-up for non-CBRN terrorism coverage. For illustration purposes, we model the loss distribution for 40 percent take-up of CBRN coverage. Results are shown in Figure 5.1.

The distribution for aircraft impact attacks is unchanged. The distribution for indoor anthrax attacks has changed little, because the majority of the losses are from workers' compensation, for which take-up is 100 percent, so the option to purchase CBRN coverage affects only a small fraction of the losses. In contrast, there is a large change in the outdoor anthrax case, where uninsured losses drop from 57 percent to 35 percent of the total. The decrease in uninsured loss is offset by an increase in loss to target insurers and taxpayers.

A potential drawback of requiring insurers to offer CBRN coverage is that it could leave individual target insurers more vulnerable to losses that exceed their payment capacity. The principal concern among insurers is that damage from a CBRN attack could span a very large geographical area and a long time duration. In other words, CBRN attacks are feared to lead to the "next asbestos," and, therefore, insurers are highly reluctant to write coverage for it. This concern is exacerbated by the limited availability of reinsurance for terrorism coverage. While the loss-sharing provision of TRIA acts as reinsurance, the fact that TRIA is in place and only about one-third of insurers have offered CBRN coverage on any policy indicates that the loss-sharing provision of TRIA does not by itself provide enough incentive for insurers to enter the CBRN coverage market. One possible explanation is that TRIA provides less flexibility for an insurer to tailor the amount of reinsurance it obtains in different markets (e.g., different geographic areas or insurance lines) than does commercial reinsurance.

Figure 5.1
Loss Distributions Estimated for Mandatory Availability of CBRN Coverage

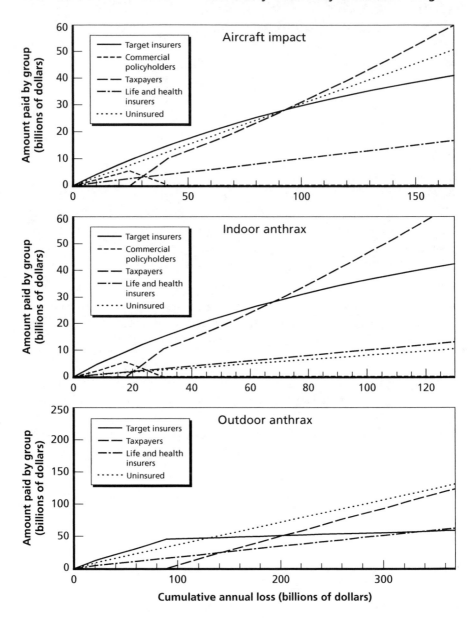

Make Terrorism Coverage Mandatory

A more radical approach to reducing uninsured losses is to mandate that all commercial policyholders insure against terrorism. It is possible that the additional premium an insurer will charge a policyholder for including terrorism coverage on a policy will cause the policyholder to decline the entire policy and go uninsured. We have no basis for estimating the extent to which that might happen and assume that such instances would be sufficiently infrequent that they can be neglected. In this case, there are no uninsured losses. (See Figure 5.2.) As with the case above, loss is transferred to target insurers and taxpayers. Mandating terrorism coverage might require the creation of a last-resort insurer for high-risk companies that could not obtain insurance from the private market.

Reduce Burden on Target Insurers: *Decrease Insurer Deductibles*

One argument for reducing the target insurers' share is to reduce the number of insurer bankruptcies after an attack and thereby preserve the overall health of the commercial insurance industry. Another argument is that decreased target insurer costs could be passed on to policyholders through decreased premiums, which could increase policyholder take-up and thereby decrease uninsured losses (see, e.g., Chalk et al., 2005). If a goal of modifying TRIA was to reduce the burden on the target insurers, the insurer deductible or co-payment must be reduced. Because in most situations an insurer's deductible will be much greater than its co-payment, a decrease in the deductible has a greater effect than an equivalent percentage decrease in the co-payment.

The effect of decreasing the deductible by a factor of two is shown in Figure 5.3. The decreased loss for target insurers is offset by an increased loss to either commercial policyholders or taxpayers, depending on the size of the loss.

Figure 5.2
Loss Distributions Estimated for Mandatory Terrorism Coverage

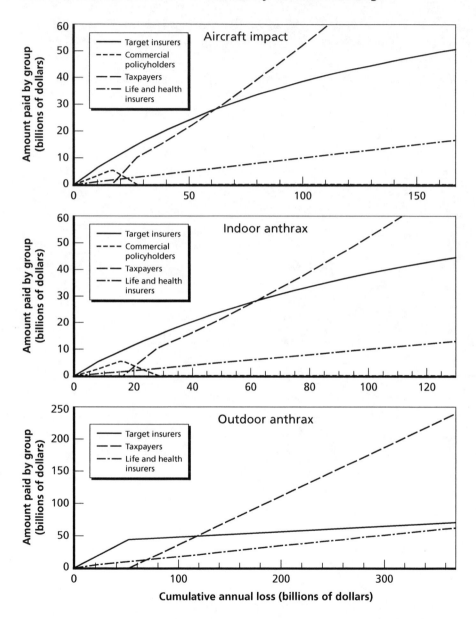

Figure 5.3
Loss Distributions Estimated for a 7.5 Percent Deductible

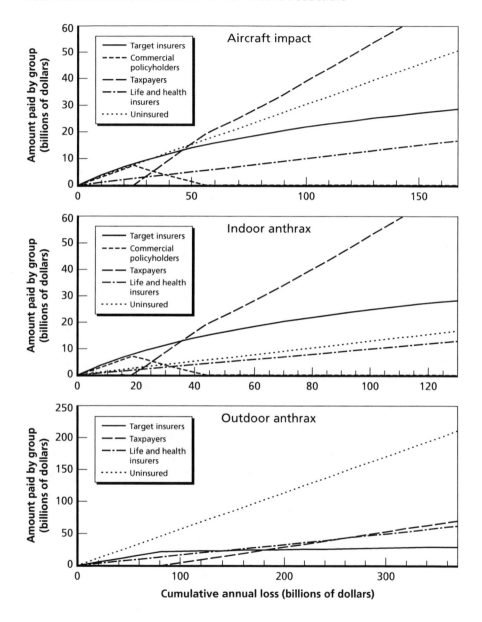

If the total loss is less than $25 billion ($20 billion) in aircraft impact (indoor anthrax) attacks, the TRIA-covered loss will be below the insurance marketplace retention level. Under these circumstances, commercial policyholders will be responsible for that share of the loss that exceeds the target insurers' deductible. Consequently, reducing the deductible shifts losses from target insurers to commercial policyholders while keeping the total insurance marketplace share constant. This option was proposed by Chalk et al. (2005) as a way to reduce terrorism insurance premiums and increase coverage take-up without increasing the burden on taxpayers. This could be a viable approach, but the burden on taxpayers would be unchanged only for losses below the insurance marketplace retention amount. For greater total loss, the sum of even the reduced aggregate deductible plus the co-payment in this example exceeds the retention. Under these circumstances, the decreased deductible is compensated for by an increase in the taxpayers' share.

Reduce Burden on Commercial Policyholders

A substantial portion of a target insurer's terrorism losses is subsidized by surcharges on commercial insurance policyholders and taxpayers. Because of this, observers have argued that insurers may have a decreased incentive to require or incentivize policyholders to implement risk-reduction measures or to develop a functioning insurance or other type of risk management market for terrorism (see, e.g., Congressional Budget Office, 2005; U.S. Department of the Treasury, 2005). The relationship between policyholder adoption of risk-reduction measures and insurance premiums, and the extent to which it is affected by TRIA, is a source of considerable controversy. This is an important and promising area for future research. One option that may be considered is to reduce this subsidy by reducing the burden on commercial policyholders or taxpayers. The burden on commercial policyholders can be reduced either by increasing the deductible or co-payment or by decreasing the insurance marketplace retention.

Increase Insurer Deductibles

The burden on commercial policyholders could be reduced by increasing either the insurer deductible or the insurer co-payment. As noted above in the section on reducing the burden on target insurers, because the effect of the deductible is generally much greater than the co-payment, an increase in the deductible has a greater effect than an equivalent percentage increase in the co-payment.

As before, if the total loss is less than $25 billion ($20 billion) in aircraft impact (indoor anthrax) attacks, the TRIA-covered loss will be below the insurance marketplace retention level. Accordingly, commercial policyholders will be responsible for that share of the loss that exceeds the target insurers' deductible. Consequently, increasing the deductible shifts losses from commercial policyholders to target insurers. Of course, if the deductible is increased above the point at which target insurers' responsibility for losses exceeds the insurance marketplace retention, commercial policyholders' responsibility for losses declines to zero, and further increases in the deductible will have no effect on commercial policyholders.

As shown in Figure 5.4, the effect on commercial policyholders of doubling the deductible is modest. A more pronounced effect of increasing the deductible is to substantially reduce the taxpayers' share.

Decrease Insurance Marketplace Retention

As long as the deductible is below the point at which target insurers' responsibility for losses exceeds the insurance marketplace retention, decreasing the retention has the effect of reducing commercial policyholders' share of total losses. If the total loss is less than $25 billion ($20 billion) in aircraft impact (indoor anthrax) attacks, the TRIA-covered loss will be below the insurance marketplace retention level. Accordingly, commercial policyholders will be responsible for that share of the loss that exceeds the target insurers' deductible. Decreasing the retention level shifts losses from commercial policyholders to taxpayers. Of course, if the retention is reduced below the point at which target insurers' responsibility for losses exceeds the insurance

Figure 5.4
Loss Distributions Estimated for a 30 Percent Deductible

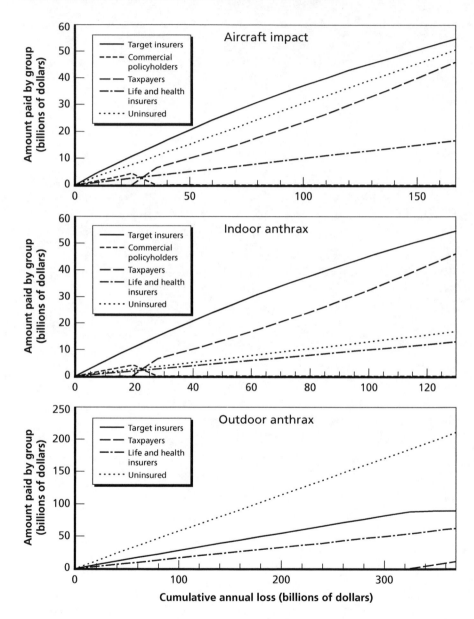

marketplace retention, commercial policyholders' responsibility for losses declines to zero, and further reductions in the retention level will have no effect on commercial policyholders. The effect of halving the retention is shown in Figure 5.5.

Reduce Burden on Taxpayers

The burden on taxpayers can be reduced either by increasing the deductible and/or the insurance marketplace retention or decreasing the aggregate ceiling on TRIA loss sharing.

Increase Deductibles and/or Insurance Marketplace Retention

The taxpayers pay the difference between TRIA-covered losses, up to $100 billion, and the sum of the target insurers' and commercial policyholders' shares. Target insurers and commercial policyholders are jointly responsible for the larger of target insurers' deductibles plus co-payments and the insurance marketplace retention. That is, under conditions when the deductible and co-payments exceed the marketplace retention (e.g., relatively large annual losses), commercial policyholders are not responsible for any of the losses, and taxpayers are responsible for the difference between total TRIA-covered losses and target insurers' responsibility. In this case, increasing the deductible (or co-payment) decreases the taxpayers' share. If the marketplace retention exceeds target insurers' responsibility (e.g., for relatively small annual losses), target insurers and commercial policyholders are responsible for the insurance marketplace retention, and taxpayers are responsible for the difference between total TRIA-covered losses and the insurance marketplace retention. Under these conditions, increasing the marketplace retention decreases the taxpayers' share. The effect of doubling the deductible is shown in Figure 5.4. The effect of doubling the insurance marketplace retention is shown in Figure 5.6.

Figure 5.5
Loss Distributions Estimated for a $7.5 Billion Retention

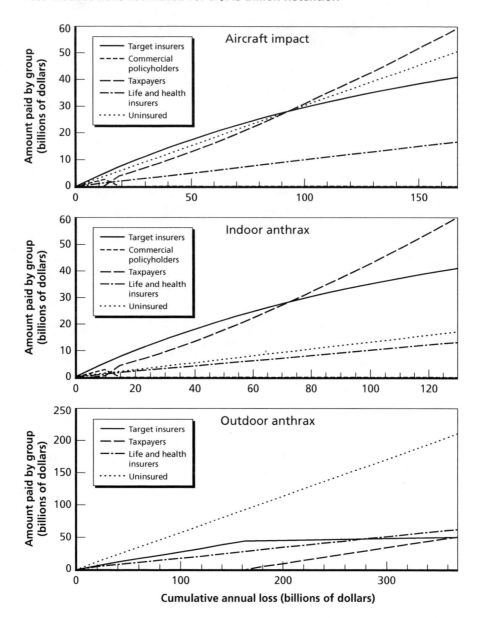

Figure 5.6
Loss Distributions Estimated for a $30 Billion Retention

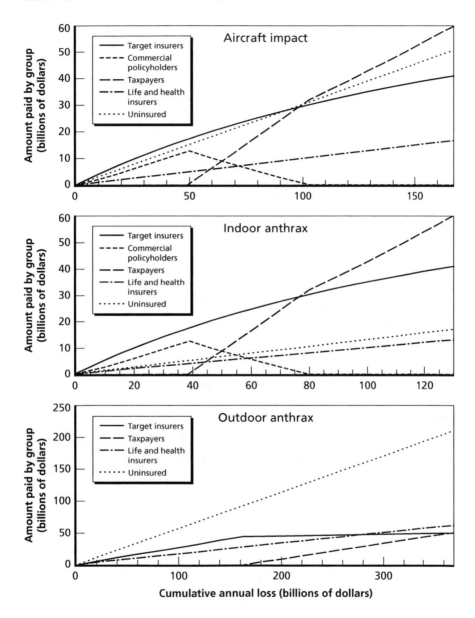

Decrease Coverage Ceiling

The taxpayers essentially pay the difference between TRIA-covered losses, up to a ceiling of $100 billion, and the target insurers' and commercial policyholders' responsibilities for those losses. Thus, taxpayers ultimately pay for TRIA-covered losses above the larger of either the sum of target insurers' deductible and co-payments or the aggregate insurance marketplace retention, up to $100 billion. If TRIA-covered losses are less than the ceiling, a reduction in the ceiling translates into a reduction in taxpayers' responsibility for the losses. The law, as currently written, does not determine whether TRIA-covered losses in excess of $100 billion will be paid and, if so, by whom. Consequently, it is not known who would become responsible for losses shifted from taxpayers by lowering the ceiling.

Summary of Alternatives

The range of possible loss distribution goals, possible modifications to TRIA to achieve those goals, and how losses are redistributed under the alternative, are summarized in Table 5.1.

Table 5.1
Distribution of Losses Under Possible Modifications to TRIA

Loss Distribution Goal	Possible Modifications	Where Losses Are Transferred
Reduce uninsured losses	Mandate CBRN coverage availability Make terrorism insurance coverage mandatory	Target insurers, commercial policyholders, and taxpayers
Reduce burden on target insurers	Decrease insurer deductibles	Commercial policyholders or taxpayers
Reduce burden on commercial policyholders	Increase insurer deductibles Decrease insurance marketplace retention	Target insurers Taxpayers

Table 5.1—continued

Reduce burden on tax-payers	Increase the deductible and/or insurance marketplace retention	Target insurers or commer-cial policyholders
	Decrease TRIA ceiling	Unknown

CHAPTER SIX

Conclusions and Implications for TRIA

The primary objective of TRIA is to maintain a viable terrorism insurance market. It attempts to do this by spreading risk of terrorism loss among several different parties to reduce the risk to any one. Through the combination of making some terrorism insurance coverage available and providing for risk spreading, TRIA influences the distribution of losses resulting from terrorist attacks among five groups: the uninsured, target insurers in lines not covered by TRIA (primarily life and health), target insurers in lines covered by TRIA, all commercial policyholders, and taxpayers. Five provisions of TRIA—insurance availability and take-up, TRIA eligibility, deductibles and co-payments, insurance marketplace retention, and the ceiling—determine how the losses resulting from terrorist attacks are redistributed.

This study presents the first comprehensive quantitative estimate of how losses from large terrorist attacks would be distributed among various stakeholders under TRIA. Because the way that TRIA distributes losses varies with insurance line and with the magnitude of losses, we find that the ultimate distribution of losses depends on the mode of those attacks and the cumulative annual losses (based on the number and size of attacks). Chapter Four discusses how losses would be distributed under TRIA among the various stakeholder groups under different circumstances.

Based on these findings, we present some general observations that are relevant to discussions regarding decisions about the pending expiration of TRIA. The first is that, under TRIA, taxpayers are unlikely to be required to contribute anything after a single large terrorist attack. The second is that, even with TRIA in place, a large fraction of losses in a terrorist attack would go uninsured. Finally, the extent to which target insurers' losses would be subsidized after an attack varies considerably with the attack mode and loss magnitude.

Taxpayer Role Under TRIA

For the specific individual attack scenarios we examined, our analysis shows that taxpayers would pay nothing under TRIA. As discussed in Chapter Four, the reason for this depends on the attack mode. In the case of the aircraft impact and indoor anthrax scenarios, the total loss (and hence TRIA-covered loss) is well below the insurance industry retention amount ($15 billion in 2005), meaning that the federal government is required to recoup 100 percent of what it pays out to target insurers. In the case of outdoor anthrax scenario, taxpayers do not contribute because the federal government never even makes an initial payout.

While we examined only three specific scenarios, we can infer from these results that taxpayers would likely not be required to contribute in any attack concentrated on a single target. Such attacks could include bombs, aircraft impacts, and most indoor biological or chemical attacks. The TRIA-covered losses in our aircraft impact and indoor anthrax attack simulations are $4.0 billion and $6.1 billion, respectively. While every attack will be different, we purposely examined cases near the high end of the expected loss range.[1] Based on these results, at least three to four very large single-target attacks would need to occur in a year before the TRIA-covered loss would reach $15 billion and taxpayers would begin to contribute.

In the case of wide-area dispersal events, such as the outdoor anthrax scenario, it is more difficult to generalize the expected taxpayer

---

[1] Recall that even in the World Trade Center attacks, we estimate that, had TRIA been in place at the time, the total TRIA-covered loss for the two impacts would have been $13 billion assuming current take-up values.

role. The total loss in our simulation coincidentally falls just below the point at which taxpayers would begin to contribute. We also examined another high-loss case and, given the range of eventualities, it is much more likely that losses from such an attack would be smaller than our estimate rather than greater. In such cases, taxpayers would not contribute. Still, while an outdoor anthrax release is considered to be among the highest-consequence types of terrorist attacks, losses for other types of attacks, particularly one with a nuclear device, could be greater. Ultimately, however, wide-area dispersal, large footprint attacks are very low probability events.

Overall, the role of taxpayers is expected to be minimal in all but very rare cases such as serial large attacks on major buildings, highly effective large outdoor anthrax releases, or nuclear detonations. An important conclusion from this finding is that TRIA is not primarily a taxpayer bailout of the insurance industry. While TRIA does provide substantial protection to insurers, in the vast majority of cases, the subsidy to target insurers under TRIA will come from surcharges on commercial policyholders rather than taxpayers in general.

An implication of this conclusion is that alternatives to TRIA need not focus on protecting taxpayers. Thus, the alternatives presented in Chapter Five designed to reduce the burden on taxpayers (increasing the deductible and/or the insurance marketplace retention and decreasing the TRIA ceiling) do not need to be high priorities. In addition, deliberations over other TRIA alternatives should discount potential adverse effects on taxpayers as long as they do not significantly decrease the point at which taxpayers begin to contribute.

We note that TRIA comprises more than a provision for a taxpayer subsidy and hence the lack of a taxpayer role does not mean that TRIA has no influence on the terrorism insurance market. Target insurers still receive substantial subsidies from the surcharge on commercial insurance policyholders, and TRIA makes property insurance for conventional terrorism available to policyholders, both of which act to make terrorism insurance more available and affordable.

It should also be noted that, even in cases where taxpayers ultimately pay nothing under the TRIA loss distribution formula, there is some indirect effect on taxpayers. First, as discussed in Chapter

Two, some fraction of the surcharge on commercial insurance policy-holders will likely ultimately be borne by the general public. In addition, even when the federal government recoups 100 percent of its initial payout, taxpayers effectively provide an interest-free loan to the target insurers because recoupment occurs in the year(s) after the event. The magnitude of these indirect effects, however, would not decrease, and in some cases would increase, if the formal taxpayers' share were reduced.

Uninsured Losses Under TRIA

As noted earlier, TRIA helps reduce uninsured terrorism losses by making coverage available and by limiting target insurers' exposure. However, our analysis shows that, even with TRIA in place, a high fraction of losses would go uninsured in each of the attack scenarios examined. Uninsured fractions range from 13 percent of the total loss in the indoor anthrax scenario to 57 percent in the outdoor anthrax scenario. The uninsured fraction is independent of total loss, meaning that there would be substantial uninsured losses in any size attack. This high uninsured loss may be considered surprising, given that a primary goal of TRIA is to bolster the terrorism insurance market by assuring the widespread availability and affordability of terrorism insurance.

To the extent that the persistence of substantial uninsured terrorism risk runs counter to the intentions of TRIA, an important consideration of modifications or alternatives to TRIA is reducing the expected uninsured losses. One option is to extend the "make-available" provision of TRIA to include CBRN attack coverage. It is difficult to predict what take-up would be if coverage were readily available; we find that, if CBRN take-up rose to 40 percent, uninsured losses in the indoor anthrax release would decrease from 13 percent to 8 percent and uninsured losses in the outdoor anthrax release would decrease from 57 percent to 35 percent. More radical approaches, such as requiring policyholders to obtain terrorism coverage, could sharply reduce or eliminate uninsured losses, but such options face a host of impediments.

Another alternative that would reduce uninsured losses is to decrease insurer deductibles or co-payments. Lower target insurer costs could be passed on to policyholders through decreased premiums, which could increase policyholder take-up. This approach directly contradicts the recommendations made by the Treasury Secretary, who stated that "[t]he Administration would accept an extension [of TRIA] only if it . . . increases the dollar deductibles and percentage co-payments" (Snow, 2005). However, as discussed in the previous section on the taxpayer role under TRIA, concerns about minimizing the government's financial responsibility under TRIA are largely unwarranted. In fact, reducing uninsured losses may ultimately reduce taxpayer liability. As demonstrated most recently with Hurricane Katrina, governments often feel compelled to compensate uninsured victims after a disaster. The expectation of post-disaster assistance can undermine the demand for insurance against future catastrophes. By facilitating the purchase of insurance, the ultimate taxpayer burden may be decreased.

Target Insurer Subsidy

A core element of TRIA is its risk-spreading formula, which limits the exposure of target insurers in a terrorist attack. After target insurers pay claims, they are partially reimbursed for their losses by funds that ultimately derive from general commercial insurance policyholders and from taxpayers.

The fact that primary target insurers' losses are subsidized has been identified as a potentially serious flaw of TRIA. According to some arguments, by subsidizing target insurer losses, TRIA attenuates the insurance industry's incentive to develop functional terrorism risk management options, including promoting risk reduction among policyholders (see, e.g., Congressional Budget Office, 2005; U.S. Department of the Treasury, 2005). The subsidy, it is argued, crowds out development of some reinsurance markets, impedes efforts to price premiums accurately and to link premium prices to risk-reduction measures, and delays the development of private capacity to absorb any future losses. In effect, the argument states that the design of TRIA actually undermines its own objective of facilitating the development of a private terrorism insurance market.

Such arguments are highly controversial. Certainly there are actions that policyholders could take to reduce their risk. At the same time, options are very limited for some types of attacks, such as an aircraft impact. More generally, however, even if the risk reduction realized from some steps could be quantified, the absolute risk of most terrorist attacks, or even the relative risk in the context of other types of disasters, remains highly uncertain, making premium pricing very difficult.

An important consideration in such arguments is the degree to which target insurer losses are subsidized. Our analysis shows that, for aircraft impact and indoor anthrax attacks, the subsidy increases from 30 percent of target insurers' loss at low total losses to 60 percent of target insurers' loss at the TRIA cap of $100 billion in TRIA-covered losses. The subsidy increases with total losses because the rate of increase in the aggregate deductible decreases with increasing total losses. As with the case for the taxpayer role discussed above, this finding is applicable more generally to any attack concentrated on a single target.

While our analysis does not provide any insight into the effect these subsidies may have on the development of a private terrorism insurance market, providing quantitative estimates of their magnitude is an important first step toward addressing this issue. At the same time, resolving this question and ultimately developing a private market will require additional research about the risk of different types of terrorist attacks and about what types of preparedness measures are available to the private sector and how effective they would be.

The Renewal of TRIA

The most relevant public policy decision regarding terrorism insurance confronting the United States is the renewal of TRIA. This study is not intended to be a comprehensive analysis of this policy decision. The analysis is limited to examining the distribution of losses across a few scenarios—not the full range of potential attacks—and has not addressed several other key considerations such as capacity of the insurance market to cover losses, the viability of reliance upon financial markets to increase capacity, national security considerations in terrorism insurance, or any number of other critical considerations. For additional research that is relevant to the renewal, see Doherty et al. (2005), Chalk et al. (2005), and Jaffee and Russell (2005), among others.

Nonetheless, our analyses do provide information that bears upon the decision regarding the renewal of TRIA. First, to the extent that taxpayer involvement is not a concern for most terrorist attacks, budgetary considerations do not seem relevant as a motivation for choosing to allow TRIA to sunset. Second, as noted by the Treasury report, allowing TRIA to sunset is likely to increase terrorism insurance premiums and lower take-up, at least initially. We have shown that there is likely to be a high fraction of uninsured losses in any future attack. To the extent that this is a policy concern, the failure to renew TRIA will contribute to this problem instead of reducing it. Finally, one of the arguments against the renewal of TRIA is that the subsidy of target insurer losses discourages efforts to price terrorism insurance and develop a private terrorism insurance market. We have shown that the extent of the subsidy differs by the type of attack, but we emphasize that the relationship between this subsidy and the development of a functional market is quite controversial and is a subject in need of greater study.

APPENDIX A

Estimating Losses and Insurance Compensation for Large Terrorist Attacks

Introduction

Because there have been no other attacks of the magnitude of the September 11th attack on the WTC, policymakers have little empirical data on which to assess the likely effects of TRIA in response to a major terrorist attack. To help inform the debate about the future of TRIA, we have simulated the expected losses from different sizes and modes of terrorist attack scenarios and examined the effects of the private insurance system on the distribution of those losses.

For this analysis, we examined the losses that would result from terrorist attacks involving aircraft impacts and indoor and outdoor anthrax releases on a number of different potential targets. We chose to examine aircraft impacts because the 9/11 aircraft impact attacks are the largest terrorist attacks in history and were the impetus for TRIA. We chose to examine CBRN terrorism because it can be very different from conventional terrorism in loss magnitude and profile. Of the various forms of CBRN, we chose anthrax for this study because it has already been used in a series of terror attacks (the mail attacks in September and October 2001), demonstrating that such an attack is within the realm of terrorists' capabilities.

The objective is to generate a realistic simulation of the losses and loss distribution in large terrorist attacks to provide the basis for estimating the effects of TRIA on the ultimate distribution of losses.

Analysis Methods

Figure A.1 summarizes our analytical approach for modeling losses and loss distributions in any particular attack scenario. We begin with an event model. The event model uses physical principles to estimate the effects of an attack on structures and people. The event model, in turn, gives rise to the attacks losses, that is, the property damage and casualties resulting from the attack. We then examine how the private insurance system would distribute these losses between insurers and policyholders and among insurance lines. The insurance model thus gives rise to the loss distribution resulting from an attack. This loss distribution then provides the basis for estimating the effects of TRIA, the results of which are discussed in the main body of this study.

Loss Estimates

Aircraft Impact. We simulated aircraft impact attacks using the Probabilistic Terrorism Model from RMS. This model provides estimates of the initial losses that would result from an aircraft impact on a specific building—not a hypothetical or reference building—within the United States.

The aircraft impact attack mode in the RMS terrorism model simulates the consequences of a fully fueled wide-body commercial aircraft impacting a tall building in a major metropolitan area. We simulated the effects of an attack on each of 454 specific targets in the United States, including every building over 40 stories tall, plus some smaller, "high-profile" buildings that have particularly high visibility or symbolic value. The buildings are generally office buildings, but

Figure A.1
Analytical Approach for Modeling Losses and Loss Distributions in an Attack Scenario

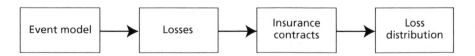

some of them are hotels, apartment buildings, or condominium complexes. In reporting results below, we show the results for both one building—referred to as "the major office building" (which is the 93rd percentile, in terms of total casualties, of the distribution of the 454 buildings)—and for all 454 buildings.

The model accounts for a number of building characteristics for each target that influence the attack consequences. These include height; number of stories; year built; construction type (masonry, steel frame, etc.); and number, occupational status, and age distribution of the occupants. Building characteristics are compiled from multiple sources, including data from the Sanborn Map Company, Inc.[1] Estimates of the number and demographics of building occupants are derived from local census data, journey-to-work data, building-use type, and building size. The number of occupants is also adjusted to account for the time of day.

The model assumes the complete collapse of the target building and accounts for damage to neighboring structures. Damage and losses from the attack occur from the spread of fire and from very high temperatures; from projectiles, embers, and debris from the collapsing structure; from smoke and dust clouds; from fatalities and injuries resulting from building collapse; and from business interruption resulting from a civil authority exclusion zone declared around the site. Separate damage and loss estimates are calculated for individual grid cells throughout the attack area based on the conditions experienced at each cell position. The impact of the attack is affected primarily by the characteristics of the target building, the time of occurrence, and the density and characteristics of the neighboring buildings.

We examined the effects of mid-afternoon, weekday attacks. Since most types of buildings would be most fully occupied at this time, our estimates reflect the worst-case scenario in the sense of the number of people exposed to the attack.

---

[1] The Sanborn Map Company, Inc., maintains extremely accurate spatial coordinates as well as numerous building attributes for buildings in major metropolitan areas in over 21 cities across the United States.

The model converts damage from the impact into losses in the form of casualties, property damage, and business interruption. The model provides estimates of the number of victims in each of six different casualty categories: medical only, temporary total disability, permanent partial minor disability, permanent partial major disability, permanent total disability, and fatality. These categories correspond to the standard workers' compensation injury categories and are defined in the same way. The model also provides estimates of the dollar value of property damage to both the building and the building contents and losses resulting from business interruption. We have also included aircraft hull losses ($125 million) based on estimates from the 9/11 attacks (Hartwig, 2004).

Business interruption losses include only losses incurred by local businesses as a result of being closed in the aftermath of the attack. For example, losses to a restaurant located near the attack site that result from the restaurant being closed, either because of damage or because it is located within an area closed by civil authorities, are covered. However, losses that result from decreased sales because fewer workers are entering the area are not included. In addition, we do not attempt to include losses incurred by non-local businesses resulting from the attack, such as losses to that restaurant's suppliers because it cut back on its purchases.

We note that there are numerous sources of uncertainty in the model results that cannot be well characterized. As a result, the actual losses in an aircraft impact could differ substantially from our model estimates. However, the analysis is not intended to develop highly accurate estimates for the consequences of an attack on any particular building. Instead, the intent is to develop estimates that can be used to explore the effects of TRIA across a broad range of eventualities. The range of losses among the 454 simulated impacts is large compared to the uncertainty of the results for any one building. Thus, for our purposes, uncertainties in the simulation modeling results are not critical problems. Because no one can accurately predict when and where terrorists will attack, TRIA, or an alternative to TRIA, must be sufficiently robust to appropriately respond to the consequences of an attack, whatever they might be.

Anthrax. As noted above, we examined indoor and outdoor anthrax attack scenarios. In both cases, we estimated casualty losses by combining an agent dispersal model with a casualty model. Casualty losses were then estimated with the RMS terrorism model. Noncasualty losses were also estimated with the RMS model.

Indoor Anthrax Release. The indoor anthrax attack scenario uses the same "major office building" that was modeled in the aircraft impact scenario. A sprayer is placed in a room on the ground floor and aerosolized dry anthrax spores are distributed throughout the building by the air circulation system. The time of release is set to 9 a.m. to maximize the number of people exposed and their time of exposure—anthrax spores can linger indoors for many hours. The intent was to produce a worst-case scenario for the number of people exposed, similar to the one we created for the aircraft impact scenario.

We assume that the release occurs undetected and that the attack is discovered three days after release. The material, equipment, and manpower required to execute an attack can easily escape detection at the time of attack. Moreover, the infected victims would take one to six days to show symptoms.[2] Consequently, we assume that anthrax is suspected through the symptoms of early patients and confirmed by laboratory tests.[3]

At the time of attack, we assume that there are 10,000 occupants in the building.[4] Because the attack is unlikely to be discovered immediately, additional people who enter the building over the three

---

[2] Analysis of the 1979 anthrax outbreak in the Soviet city of Sverdlovsk has indicated a much longer incubation period—perhaps as long as 43 days. However, our analysis of the 2001 mail attacks in the United States has indicated that the Soviet data are not compatible with the 2001 results, and the one-to-six-day estimate for the incubation period of inhalational anthrax is to be preferred. See Chow et al., n.d., and Appendix B.

[3] Note that in a covert attack, it may be difficult to identify the perpetrators, since they would be far from the scene well before the attack was recognized. This would complicate the application of TRIA, which requires that for an attack to qualify for cost sharing, the perpetrators must be acting for a "foreign person or foreign interest."

[4] The building under consideration is about as large as one of the World Trade Center towers. The maximum capacity of these towers was about 25,000 people per tower. On the morning of September 11, 2001, WTC 1 was thought to contain between 8,150 to 9,650 people, and WTC 2 was thought to contain between 7,620 to 9,460 people (NIST, 2005).

days subsequent to the attack will also be exposed. Although the anthrax spores would have settled out of the air within several hours of the release, new building entrants could still be affected in two ways. First, some could inhale re-aerosolized spores that were stirred up by human or mechanical movements in the building. Second, some could contract cutaneous anthrax by coming into contact with spores that had settled on surfaces. We estimated that 4,250 of the subsequent entrants would be affected before the attack is detected and the building is closed.

We model the distribution of anthrax throughout the building and the dose level by floor with the CONTAMW Multizone Airflow and Contaminant Transport Model from the National Institute of Standards and Technology (Dols and Walton, 2002). This model is capable of simulating the dispersal of aerosols and gasses in complex indoor environments. In particular, the model can account for the design of a building's air-handling system, including the number of separate circulation zones and the filtering efficiency. Once the chemical or biological agent, building floor plan, air-handling system, and the environmental conditions are specified, the model will simulate the aerosol release from a given indoor location and output the dose at a given time, as well as the cumulative dose over time at any indoor location.

For our analysis, we modeled a 50-story building, with each floor having an open floor plan (i.e., there were no interior office partitions or corridors). One air outlet and return was used per floor. We performed excursions using floors with multiple interior offices, air outlets, and returns, but they made little difference to the result. We assumed a single air-handling system for the entire building (i.e., a single zone). We performed excursions using two separate systems (one for each half of the building) and found that under certain environmental conditions the casualties could be significantly reduced. Under many conditions, however, having separate systems did not change the number of casualties. Given this possibility, we model a single air-handling system in this analysis. We assume that the air on each floor is recirculated at a rate of 5 percent per minute and that 15 percent of this air was replaced by outside air during each pass through the system. We also estimated parameters for building window and door air leakage, as well as the indoor and outdoor environmental conditions.

The results from our 50-story building were scaled to match the size of the target building under consideration (i.e., the "major office building" discussed above).

Outdoor Anthrax Release. For the outdoor anthrax release scenario, we assume the terrorists target a highly populated, metropolitan downtown area. A sprayer mounted on a moving truck releases 75 kilograms of anthrax-containing slurry as it drives along a 5-kilometer linear path. As in the indoor release case, the release takes place at 9 a.m. to catch workers at the beginning of their workday and maximize their time of exposure.

In contrast to the aircraft impact and indoor anthrax scenarios, the footprint of the outdoor anthrax release is several hundred square kilometers. The anthrax spore density as a function of location and time was modeled with the Chemical/Biological Agent Vapor, Liquid, and Solid Tracking (VLSTRACK) model (Bauer and Gibbs, 2001). We modeled the population density in the affected area in four concentric zones: 20,000 persons per square kilometer in a 4 kilometer by 5 kilometer downtown area, 5,000 persons per square kilometer extending out to 25 kilometers, 1,000 persons per square kilometer out to 65 kilometers, and zero population beyond 65 kilometers.

Most of the casualties would take place inside buildings, since there are typically many more people indoors than outdoors. In our scenario, we assume all the casualties occur indoors. To determine indoor dose levels, we first used the VLSTRACK model to estimate the outdoor dose levels at various locations and heights above ground where building air inlets are located, then used the CONTAMW model to estimate the reduction in dose that would occur as the spores pass through the building air filtration system.

Any downtown would have buildings with their air inlets located at various heights. In a release from a ground sprayer, the dose would be lower as the height above the ground increases. For the downtown area, we assume that 50 percent of the population would inhale a dose from the contaminated air entering the building at a 2-meter level, 30 percent receive a lesser dose from air inlets at a 100-meter height, and 20 percent from a 200-meter height. Beyond the downtown area, anthrax enters all buildings at ground level. In estimating the indoor dose levels, we assume that the downtown buildings are protected by 60 percent efficient filters and that buildings outside the downtown area do not have filters that have efficiency of any significance (thus, in effect, no filter). Persons in the buildings with 60 percent efficient filters have a factor of nine reduction in the dose when compared with that received by persons outside the building.[5] Persons in the buildings with no filters receive the same dose as that experienced by persons outside the building.

Casualties from Anthrax Attacks. For both indoor and outdoor anthrax attacks, we used an expanded version of a casualty model developed at RAND to convert the cumulative anthrax dose level at any location into a distribution of casualties at various injury levels (Chow et al., n.d.; see Appendix B for details.) Because we use the RMS model to estimate insured losses from casualties, we use the RMS injury classifications described above. However, in this case, the casualty model assigns victims of an anthrax attack into only four of the six injury levels; the model assumes there will be no permanent partial disabilities. As discussed in detail in Appendix B, inhalational anthrax has an incubation period of one to six days and a prodromal phase, where the victims show initial mild symptoms, that lasts for one to seven days. The casualty distribution from an anthrax attack is very sensitive to the timing of medical intervention, and for this analysis we assume that it takes three days to detect the attack and another day for effective medical treatments and prophylaxis to begin (see Appendix B).

Because documented case histories of anthrax victims are sparse, there is substantial uncertainty about the injury distribution that can be expected in an attack. A year after illness onset, six survivors from

---

[5] The released anthrax spores would make multiple passes through the filters as the air is recirculated in the building, which is why the reduction factor is large relative to the efficiency of the filter.

inhalational anthrax and eleven from cutaneous anthrax incurred during 2001 were run through a battery of health assessments and many were found to have chronic cough, fatigue, joint swelling and pain, memory problems, abnormalities in pulmonary functions, etc. They also exhibited psychological symptoms, such as depression, anxiety, and phobias, and were in reduced health in terms of physical functioning, bodily pain, and mental health (Reissman et al., 2004). Moreover, five of the six inhalational anthrax survivors had not returned to work after at least two years (Shane, 2003).

The traditional definition of permanent disability focuses on traumatic structural injuries; yet major components of disability resulting from anthrax appear to be chronic physical and psychological impairments. Given the very small sample size from the anthrax attacks and the fact that these cases are still progressing, it is unclear to what extent these cases will constitute temporary or permanent disabilities. We account for this uncertainty by examining two casualty distribution cases. In the "low permanent total disability" case, we assume that the ratio of temporary total to permanent total disabilities is 3 to 1, and in the "high permanent total disability" case, we use a ratio of 1 to 3. These two cases are intended to bracket the likely outcomes of a population exposed to anthrax (see Appendix B for further discussion).

Non-Casualty Losses from Anthrax Attacks. Non-casualty losses from indoor and outdoor anthrax attacks were estimated with the RMS terrorism model and include building, contents, and business interruption losses. Building losses in an anthrax attack result from decontamination costs. Given the very limited number of buildings that have been decontaminated after an anthrax release, none of which were pervasively contaminated as would be the case in the scenario modeled here, estimates of decontamination costs are highly uncertain. Consequently, we also examine a case where the building is condemned and use the replacement value for the building loss. Contents losses are a combination of decontamination and replacement, and business interruption losses are estimated in the same manner as for an aircraft impact attack.

Limitations of Loss Estimates

The event modeling captures the major losses anticipated from the different types of attacks simulated. However, because of limitations in available data, some important categories of losses are not accounted for. First, losses to government workers—including emergency responders and government buildings—are not included in the RMS database and, thus, are not considered in our analysis. Excluding these workers and buildings will have little impact on the subsequent analyses of how TRIA will affect the distribution of losses resulting from a terrorist attack, because government workers and buildings are (self)insured by governmental agencies, not private insurers; thus, these losses are not affected by TRIA.

Another limitation is that the model accounts for victims in only three types of locations: work, home, or school. Therefore, the analysis does not account for potential attack victims who are neither employees or residents, such as visitors, clients, tourists, or passersby. The fraction of non-employee victims in the 9/11 attacks is unknown, but in attacks targeting individual commercial buildings, this fraction is likely to be much less than 10 percent. Non-employee victims of an attack, or their survivors, may be compensated by life and/or health insurance. Hence, while including non-employee victims would increase the overall loss estimate slightly, the addition would be in life and health insurance lines, which are not included under TRIA. Therefore, the exclusion of these victims does not affect analyses of the distribution of losses under TRIA.

The model also excludes non-commercial property, including single family homes and small apartment buildings. This exclusion has no effect on the aircraft impact and indoor anthrax attacks, but it will lead to an underestimation of the decontamination costs in the outdoor anthrax attack scenario. This exclusion means that the property decontamination costs estimated for an outdoor anthrax attack, which are expected to be very high (see below), must be considered lower limits.

In addition, the model also does not consider aircraft passengers and crew for aircraft impact attacks. In a large attack, these individuals will represent a small fraction of the total loss.

Moreover, while the model accounts for direct business interruption losses resulting from business closures, we do not attempt to estimate the indirect economic effects, and consequent losses, of an attack. For example, we do not attempt to estimate the losses incurred by hotels, airlines, venues, etc. subsequent to an attack as a result of the cancellation of events in the city in which an attack occurs.

Finally, we do not consider in this analysis non-insurance compensation mechanisms, such as the 9/11 Victims' Compensation Fund and the liability system. The 9/11 Victims' Compensation Fund was not enacted as a permanent program, so we cannot be sure whether something analogous would be instituted in response to a future attack and, if so, what its characteristics would be; thus, we omit it. While liability losses may be significant,[6] none of the pending suits from the 9/11 attack have been resolved, and there is tremendous uncertainty about the outcomes of these suits. Further, Congress limited airlines' liability for losses that resulted from the 9/11 attack to their insurance coverage and offered victims of that attack compensation through the 9/11 Victims' Compensation Fund in return for their waiving their liability rights. Accordingly, a large number of liability claims that might have been brought in the wake of 9/11 were essentially preempted. Whether and, if so, how Congress might act to limit liability in future attacks is unknown. In sum, we do not have a basis for estimating either the numbers and types of liability claims that might be filed in a future event or the likely outcomes of claims that are filed. Accordingly, we omit potential liability losses from this analysis.

Loss Distribution Estimates

For all three types of attacks, we used the RMS model to estimate how losses would be distributed among various insurance lines through the private-sector insurance system. Our estimates of insured loss neglect insurance premiums, deductibles, co-payments, and pol-

---

[6] The Insurance Information Institute estimates that non-aviation liability costs from 9/11 could be $10 billion (Hartwig, 2002).

icy limits. This simplification shifts losses that would be incurred by policyholders to insurers and allows us to eliminate policyholders as a separate payee. This results in a slight overestimation of the insurers' share of losses, but it has no effect on the total loss estimate.

We estimate commercial property losses under the hypothetical condition of 100 percent coverage. In particular, we neglect policy exclusions for losses resulting from CBRN attacks. We model 100 percent coverage in an effort to capture the total loss from an attack. The effect of incomplete insurance coverage take-up on the ultimate distribution of losses is examined in the main body of this report.

The RMS model distinguishes three general classes of insurance in terms of how losses are distributed: commercial property, workers' compensation, and life and health. Commercial property comprises non-casualty losses and includes buildings, building contents, and business interruption. Because we omit policy deductibles, co-payments, and limits, losses for buildings damaged or destroyed in an attack equal the buildings' full replacement value. Contents and business interruption losses are estimated at average insured values. As noted above, business interruption losses are estimated for closed, local businesses only.

Injuries and fatalities generate losses through workers' compensation and various life and health insurance lines. We assume that workers injured at their place of work are compensated at the workers' compensation rate in the state in which they were injured, given their injuries. Because workers' compensation coverage is mandatory, losses to all workers are captured in this estimate. Workers and non-workers injured or killed in an attack are compensated by various forms of life and health insurance at national average penetration rates and coverage levels by insurance line and type of population. For example, we assume that 60 percent of employed professionals have individual life insurance at an average coverage of $150,000.[7]

---

[7] Penetration rates and coverage levels for some target areas such as New York City likely exceed national averages; thus, the model may underestimate life and health insurance losses in such areas. However, this underestimation has a small effect on the conclusions of this

The total loss estimates reflected in the loss distributions are intended to represent the losses from a terrorist attack that could potentially be covered by insurance. This includes the replacement value of all damaged commercial buildings and contents; losses to businesses that are closed; workers' compensation payments for all employees; and life and health insurance payments for employees, residents, and students reflecting average insurance penetration rates and coverage levels. As noted above, some important losses are not accounted for. The principal insurable losses that are not included in our estimates are life and health insurance losses for victims who are not at work, home, or school and non-commercial property losses in an outdoor anthrax attack.

Aircraft Impact Results

In this section, we present the aircraft impact results. We conducted aircraft impact simulations for each of 454 target scenarios. To illustrate the simulation analysis, we first present detailed results for one particular scenario—the "major office building" scenario that is in the 93rd percentile of the distribution of the 454 buildings; then, we examine the range of losses across all the scenarios.

Loss Estimate and Distribution for the Major Office Building

Table A.1 summarizes the private-sector losses and loss distribution we estimate in the major office building aircraft impact scenario. Empty cells reflect those areas that are not applicable. The estimates for each line of workers' compensation, life, and health insurance are presented in two columns. The first column shows the number of people in each casualty category that we estimate would receive compensation through that line of insurance. The second column shows the total compensation that we estimate would be paid to people in that casualty category under that line of insurance. Note that an indi-

analysis, since life and health insurance losses are a relatively small fraction of the total loss, and life and health insurance is not covered by TRIA.

Table A.1
Loss Distribution for an Aircraft Impact on the Major Office Building

Loss Type	Group Life		Individual Life		Accidental Death and Dismemberment		Workers' Compensation		Health		Property	Total	
	No.	$M	No.	$M	No.	$M	No.	$M	No.	$M	$M	No.	$M
Medical only							35,169	23	186	0		35,524	23
Temporary total disability							638	8	1	0		641	8
Permanent partial disability—minor							558	14	1	0		561	14
Permanent partial disability—major					197	4	399	85	1	0		401	89
Permanent total disability					211	9	428	491	1	1		430	501
Fatal	2,224	307	1,569	235	1,306	108	2,624	901	2	0		2,632	1,551
Non-casualty													
Building											1,693	1,693	
Contents											975	975	
Business interruption											1,689	1,689	
Aircraft hull											125	125	
Total	2,224	307	1,569	235	1,714	121	39,816	1,522	192	1	4,482	40,188	6,668

NOTE: Empty cells reflect those areas that are not applicable.

vidual may be covered by more than one insurance line. Consequently, the sum of numbers of people listed in a given casualty category may be greater than the total number of people who incurred an
injury in that category shown in the "Total" column.

The "Property" column shows our estimates of non-casualty
losses. The target building and neighboring structures would incur an
estimated $4.5 billion in losses to the structures and contents and in
business interruption.

The last pair of columns shows the totals for the numbers of
people and compensation for each loss category. We estimate that
there are about 40,000 total casualties and a total loss of $6.7 billion
for this scenario. The corresponding loss for the World Trade Center
attacks on 9/11 was approximately $22 billion, or $11 billion for
each of the two impacts.[8]

Figure A.2 shows the estimated number of casualties in each of
the six casualty categories shown in Table 3.1. Most of the casualties
that would be incurred as a result of an aircraft impact are relatively
minor. Of the approximately 40,000 casualties, 88 percent fall into
the medical-only category. Most of the remaining casualties are fatalities (7 percent), with the total for the four intermediate categories
contributing just about 5 percent. As the figure shows, the casualty
profile for an aircraft impact is bimodal: Most casualties are either
minor or fatal, with relatively few casualties falling in between.

Figure A.3 shows the estimated losses for each of the six casualty
categories. Because the more serious types of casualties involve much
higher costs, the financial losses associated with casualties are dominated by fatalities. Although the number of fatalities is less than 10
percent of the number of medical-only casualties, the total losses that
would be paid to their families and estates would be over $1.5 billion,
or more than 67 times higher than the medical-only costs.

Figure A.4 shows the distribution of estimated losses among the
different insurance lines. Losses are not concentrated in any single

---

[8] The $22 billion value for the World Trade Center losses includes property, aircraft hull,
business interruption, event cancellation, workers' compensation, and life but excludes potential liability losses (Hartwig, 2004).

Figure A.2
Estimated Number of Casualties for the Major Office Building Aircraft
Impact Scenario

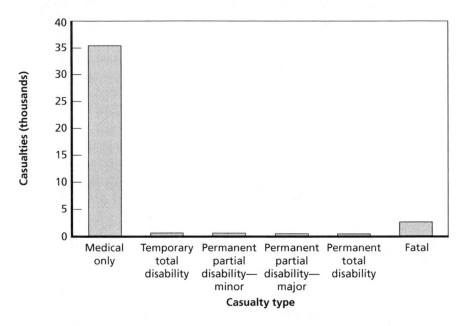

insurance line, but rather are distributed across several lines. Replacement costs for buildings and contents would account for the largest portion, totaling approximately $2.7 billion. Business interruption losses for closed businesses would be $1.7 billion. Workers' compensation losses would add up to almost as much, about $1.5 billion. Life and health, the term we use for the sum of all types of life and health insurance aside from workers' compensation, would account for a little over $600 million. The aircraft hull would cost about $125 million.

For comparison, the corresponding losses for the World Trade Center attacks are also shown in Figure A.4. To facilitate comparison to the single impact in our simulation, the World Trade Center values shown are half of the totals given by Hartwig (2004). Note that we did not simulate an impact into the World Trade Center, so our loss estimates are not expected to match the World Trade Center

Figure A.3
**Estimated Losses by Casualty Category for the Major Office Building Aircraft
Impact Scenario**

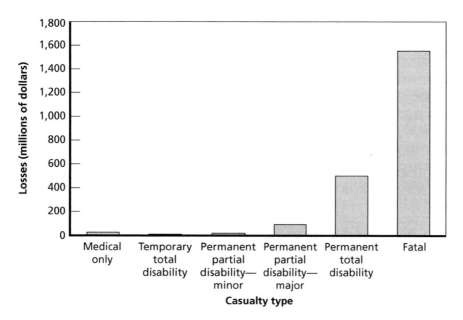

losses. Nonetheless, it is informative to understand how other large
aircraft impact attacks might compare to the World Trade Center.

Life and health and workers' compensation losses in our major
office building simulation are somewhat higher than the World Trade
Center values. This difference may reflect a larger number of victims
as well as a higher workers' compensation rate for the state in which
our simulated building is located. Property losses are considerably
higher for the World Trade Center, which is not surprising given that
they were among the most valuable buildings in the country. Business
interruption losses at the World Trade Center were almost three
times higher than in our simulation, which probably reflects the very
high density of large businesses in lower Manhattan as well as the fact
that our simulation may not capture all business interruption losses.

Figure A.5 compares insured casualty losses to non-casualty
losses estimated from the model. Casualty losses include workers'

Figure A.4
Distribution of Estimated Losses Among Different Insurance Lines for the Major Office Building Aircraft Impact Scenario and World Trade Center

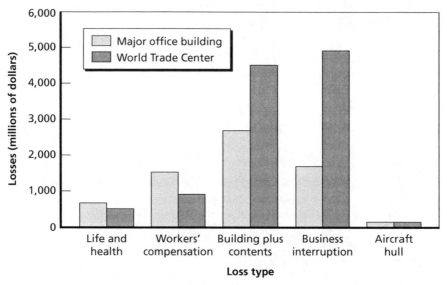

SOURCE: For WTC, estimates are half the totals from Hartwig (2004).

compensation and life and health lines, while non-casualty losses in-clude the buildings, their contents, business interruption, and aircraft hull. In this particular aircraft impact scenario, the total losses are dominated by non-casualty losses. Of the total of almost $7 billion in losses, roughly two-thirds, or about $4.5 billion, would be non-casualty losses, primarily losses due to business interruption and losses to the building. Casualty losses of all types combined add up to a lit-tle under one-third of all the losses. Most of these are the losses to workers' compensation, about $1.5 billion. All the life and health plans combined add up to a little over half a billion dollars.

Loss Estimates and Distributions for All 454 Aircraft Impact Scenarios
As noted above, we replicated the analysis for 454 independent air-craft impact scenarios involving different target buildings. The pre ceding charts described the initial losses and private-sector loss distri-

Figure A.5
Comparison of Casualty Losses to Non-Casualty Losses for the Major Office Building Aircraft Impact Scenario

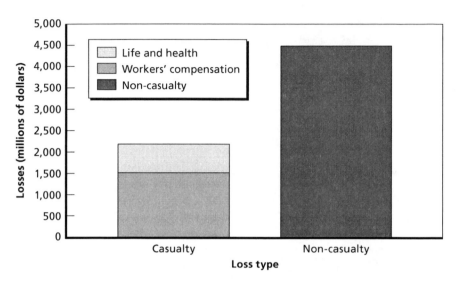

bution for a single aircraft impact scenario involving a major office building. In the next few figures, we explore how the losses and loss distribution vary among all 454 aircraft impact scenarios. The sample is comprised of actual buildings and includes all buildings in the United States over 40 stories tall, as well as a number of other high-profile or otherwise high-risk buildings.

Figure A.6 shows the distribution of the number of total casualties for attacks at the different targets. The total number of casualties ranges from less than 100 to over 60,000. Target buildings are listed in order of their percentile within the entire sample. For the target representing the 10th percentile, for example, 10 percent of all targets resulted in fewer casualties and 90 percent resulted in larger numbers of casualties. The major office building we used in the preceding figures to illustrate our analysis falls at the 93rd percentile in this distribution.

Figure A.6
Distribution of the Number of Total Casualties for All 454 Aircraft Impact Scenarios

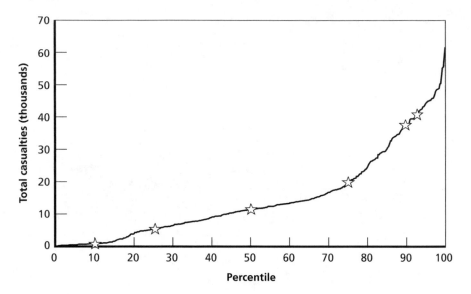

Targets at the 10th, 25th, 50th, 75th, and 90th percentile, as well as the major office building at the 93rd percentile, are highlighted with stars. In the subsequent figures, we describe and compare the results for these different target buildings.

Figure A.7 shows the total losses for three different targets at each of six casualty percentile levels highlighted in Figure A.6. The three targets shown at each percentile level are the target at that level plus the one immediately below it and the one immediately above it. The figure illustrates that the magnitude of losses varies substantially across targets. The total losses for the 18 scenarios illustrated range from $0.5 billion to $6.7 billion.

There are even notable variations in total losses among targets with very similar total casualties. For example, the three targets that bracket the 10th percentile in total casualties would incur total losses ranging from about $300 million to about $750 million. The wide range in total losses results from a combination of factors, including building height, construction type, occupancy, and location.

Figure A.7
Distribution of Total Loss Estimates for All 454 Aircraft Impact Scenarios

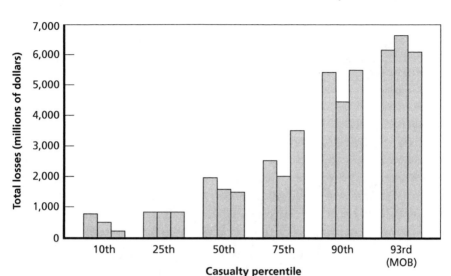

The distribution of estimated losses across different loss types also varies substantially. Figure A.8 shows the share of the total losses for each target that would be covered by each of three major types of insurance: life and health, workers' compensation, and commercial property (non-casualty). This figure illustrates that the profile of losses varies substantially across these buildings, particularly for the targets with the lowest losses. For example, almost all the losses in the 10th percentile targets are non-casualty losses. In contrast, most losses in the 25th percentile targets are from workers' compensation, with less than 30 percent of the losses resulting from non-casualty lines.[9] Targets above the 25th percentile show much more consistent distributions intermediate between these two cases. The variations result primarily from differences in property values, workers' compensation rates, and numbers of victims.

---

[9] Results for the three buildings at the 25th percentile are identical because they happen to be three identical buildings. The high ratio of workers' compensation to property loss for these buildings results from a combination of them being in a state with exceptionally high workers' compensation rates and of them having anomalously low property value.

Figure A.8
Distribution of the Total Losses Across Different Loss Types for a Sample of
the 454 Aircraft Impact Scenarios

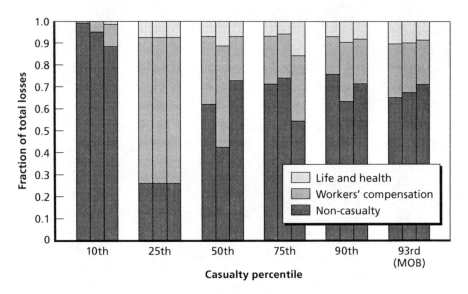

Figure A.8 also shows that the life and health insurer losses total less than 16 percent and, in most cases, less than 10 percent of the total losses. This is an important observation because life and health lines are not covered by TRIA. The fact that life and health insurance losses can be expected to represent no more than about 10–15 percent of the total losses means that the majority of the losses in an aircraft impact attack would be eligible for TRIA coverage.

Loss Estimates and Distributions for Indoor and Outdoor Anthrax Attacks

Table A.2 summarizes the results for the losses in an indoor anthrax release in the major office building. As discussed above, loss estimates presented in this study are intended to reflect the total loss that could potentially be insured. As such, CBRN exclusions, as well as any other policy deductibles, co-payments, and limits are omitted. The

Table A.2
Loss Distribution for the Major Office Building Indoor Anthrax Attack

	Group Life		Individual Life		Accidental Death and Dismemberment		Workers' Compensation		Health		Property	Total	
	No.	$M	No.	$M	No.	$M	No.	$M	No.	$M	$M	No.	$M
Medical only							5,500	3	0	0		5,500	3
Low PTD case													
Temporary total disability							4,500	54	0	0		4,500	54
Permanent total disability					738	31	1,497	1,717	3	3		1,500	1,752
High PTD case													
Temporary total disability							1,500	18	0	0		1,500	18
Permanent total disability					2,213	94	4,490	5,150	10	10		4,500	5,255
Fatal	2,336	323	1,649	247	1,374	114	2,749	944	1	0		2,750	1,628
Building											307		307
Contents											230		230
Business interruption											524		524
Total: low PTD case	2,336	323	1,649	247	2,112	145	14,246	2,717	4	3	1,061	14,250	4,498
Total: high PTD case	2,336	323	1,649	247	3,587	208	14,239	6,115	11	10	1,061	14,250	7,965

NOTES: PTD = permanent total disability. Empty cells reflect those areas that are not applicable.

total loss would be $4.5 billion for the low-permanent-total-disability case and nearly $8 billion for the high-permanent-total-disability case (see above and Appendix B for a discussion of the high- and low-permanent-total-disability cases). These values bracket the $6.7 billion for the loss caused by an aircraft impact into the same major office building, as discussed above. Thus, indoor anthrax and aircraft impact attacks are expected to inflict comparable total losses.

Table A.3 shows the comparable results for the outdoor anthrax attack scenario, again under the assumption that CBRN coverage is not excluded. Our estimate of the total insured loss ranges from $130 billion to $170 billion in the two cases. This is far greater than the losses in the indoor anthrax and aircraft impact scenarios as well as the $22 billion insured loss suffered at the World Trade Center on 9/11 (Hartwig, 2004). Such a result is to be expected given that the outdoor anthrax attack covers hundreds of square kilometers and exposes over 1.1 million people.

Turning now to casualties from the two scenarios, Figure A.9 shows the number of casualties in each injury category for the indoor anthrax attack. All 10,000 of the people in the building at the time of the attack are exposed to an anthrax dose high enough so that all of them would develop inhalational anthrax if no prophylaxis were used. Additionally 4,250 subsequent entrants are also affected. As discussed above, our casualty model places casualties in four injury levels: medical only, temporary total disability, permanent total disability, and fatal. There would be 5,500 victims at the medical-only level. As discussed above and in more detail in Appendix B, the majority of medical-only casualties are potentially exposed people who receive antibiotic prophylaxis in time to prevent any illness.[10] The estimated number of fatalities (2,750) is very similar to that for the aircraft impact simulation (2,632; see Table A.1) and the sum from the two

---

[10] The 5,500 are broken down as follows: 2,500 are people who were in the building at the time of the attack and would have developed inhalational anthrax but do not because of antibiotic prophylaxis; 2,500 are people who take antibiotic prophylaxis but in fact do not really need to; and 500 are people with mild cases of cutaneous anthrax who can be treated as outpatients.

Table A.3
Loss Distribution for the Outdoor Anthrax Attack

	Group Life		Individual Life		Accidental Death and Dismemberment		Workers' Compensation		Health		Property		Total	
	No.	$M	No.	$M	No.	$M	No.	$M	No.	$M	No.	$M	No.	$M
Low PTD case														
Medical only							479,221	308	407,827	228			1,041,370	536
Temporary total disability							30,298	363	21,441	136			59,881	499
Permanent total disability					4,979	212	10,099	11,586	7,147	7,147			19,960	18,945
High PTD case														
Medical only							875,027	562	744,665	417			1,901,476	979
Temporary total disability							10,099	121	7,147	45			19,960	166
Permanent total disability					14,936	637	30,298	34,757	21,441	21,441			59,881	56,835
Fatal	23,894	2,472	15,904	2,109	11,321	846	23,401	8,032	9,546	451			36,594	13,909
Building												32,605		32,605
Contents												22,944		22,944
Business interruption												44,864		44,864
Total: low PTD case	23,894	2,472	15,904	2,109	16,300	1,058	543,019	20,288	445,961	7,963		100,414	1,157,805	134,302
Total: high PTD case	23,894	2,472	15,904	2,109	26,258	1,483	938,825	43,472	782,800	22,354		100,414	2,017,911	172,302

NOTES: PTD = permanent total disability. Empty cells reflect those areas that are not applicable.

Figure A.9
Estimated Number of Casualties for the Major Office Building Indoor Anthrax Attack Scenario

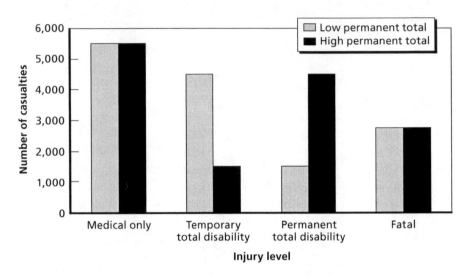

World Trade Center towers (*The 9/11 Commission Report,* 2004).[11] Many survivors of serious anthrax illness (6,000 total) could become permanently disabled: 1,500 to 4,500 for the low- and high-permanent-total-disability cases, respectively.[12] The corresponding numbers at the temporary total disability level are 4,500 and 1,500.

Figure A.10 shows the comparable casualties result for the outdoor attack scenario. Because of the very large areal extent of an outdoor anthrax release, 1,160,000 people are inside the plume, and as a result, the expected number of casualties is much greater than for an

---

[11] The 2,750 fatalities are broken down as follows: 2,500 who were in the building at the time of the attack and 250 who enter the building sometime after the attack and contract inhalational anthrax as a result of re-aerosolized anthrax.

[12] These 6,000 survivors of serious anthrax illness are broken down as follows: 5,000 who are in the building at the time of the attack and develop inhalation anthrax, 500 subsequent entrants who develop inhalational anthrax as a result of re-aerosolized anthrax, and 500 subsequent entrants who develop cases of cutaneous anthrax severe enough to be hospitalized.

Figure A.10
Estimated Number of Casualties for the Outdoor Anthrax Attack in a Major Urban Area

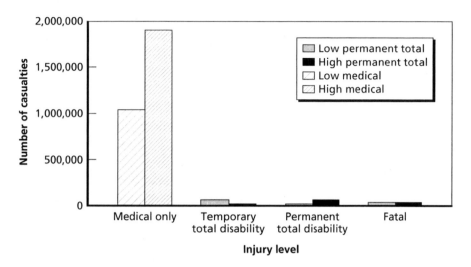

indoor release.[13] In our scenario, approximately 133,000 people would be infected, leading to 37,000 fatalities. The relative proportions of temporary total disability, permanent total disability, and fatal casualties would be the same as in the indoor case, but the number of medical-only casualties would be far greater and far more uncertain (see Appendix B). Because of the large number of people receiving antibiotic prophylaxis, the number of victims requiring medical-only care overwhelms the rest, ranging from 1.0 to 1.9 million (Figure A.10).

_____

[13] The plume size is defined as the area receiving an anthrax dose that has a chance of greater than 2 percent to infect unprophylaxed people.

Figure A.11
Estimates for Casualty Losses for the Major Office Building Indoor Anthrax Attack

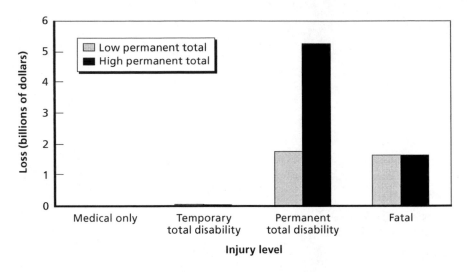

Figure A.11 shows estimates for the insured casualty losses in each of the four injury levels for the indoor anthrax attack.[14] The losses are dominated by permanent total disability and fatal injuries. Because the cost of taking care of a permanently totally disabled person ($900,000 to $2,100,000) is even higher than that of compensating the family for a death ($140,000 to $750,000), permanent total disability could be the largest share of the casualty loss. In the high-permanent-total-disability case, the permanent total disability loss would be $5.3 billion, far exceeding the $1.6 billion for the fatal loss.

When casting casualties in terms of insured monetary values for the outdoor anthrax scenario, we find that, as in the indoor scenario,

---

[14] We use RMS data to translate the casualty numbers into monetary casualty losses. RMS provided the following cost range per person: $400 to $1,000 for medical only; $16,000 to $34,000 for temporary total disability; $900,000 to $2,100,000 for permanent total disability; and $140,000 to $750,000 for fatal. RMS uses compensation rates in the state in which the victims are injured. It further assumes that the rate at a given injury level is independent of the cause of injury. Given the paucity of specific rate data for anthrax, this assumption of independence is used here.

casualty losses are dominated by permanent disabilities and fatalities (see Figure A.12). Although the number of medical-only victims overwhelms those of the other injury levels, the medical-only cost per victim is much lower than for other casualties.[15] The loss in permanent total disability ranges from $19 billion to $57 billion, and fatality loss is $14 billion. The medical-only and temporary-total-disability losses combined amount to less than $1.5 billion.

Because the cost of indemnifying permanent disabilities is so much higher than that for temporary disabilities, the large uncertainty about the relative proportion of temporary and permanent disabilities leads to large uncertainty in the total casualty loss. Thus, it is important for future research to study inhalational anthrax survivors to accurately characterize the long-term medical effects of anthrax to help classify the seriously ill into temporary and permanent disability categories.

Figure A.12
Estimates for Casualty Losses for the Outdoor Anthrax Attack in a Major Urban Area

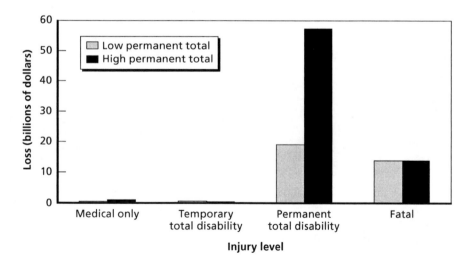

---

[15] In estimating losses by casualty type, we have grouped the high-medical-only case with the high-permanent-total-disability case and the low-medical-only case with the low-permanent-total-disability case.

Figure A.13 shows the losses for several important insurance lines for the indoor anthrax scenario. Workers' compensation dominates the losses among insurance lines. It ranges from $2.7 billion to $6.1 billion, while the other lines combined amount to $1.8 billion to $1.9 billion. This scenario calls for special attention because insurers cannot exclude CBRN coverage from workers' compensation policies. In other words, even if CBRN coverage is excluded from other lines, insurers would still be responsible for covering the bulk of the losses in an indoor anthrax attack.

Life and health insurer losses, which include group life, individual life, accidental death and dismemberment, and health insurance, amount to $0.7 billion to $0.8 billion. The building loss results mainly from decontamination expenses, which amount to $0.3 billion. Then again, if it is determined that the building cannot be decontaminated and has to be written off, it would cost $1.7 billion. As to contents, they would be decontaminated whenever possible; otherwise, they would have to be replaced. They amount to $0.2 billion. The business interruption is caused by the shutdown of business at the building until it is decontaminated and amounts to $0.5 billion.

Figure A.13
Distribution of Insured Losses Across Insurance Lines for the Major Office Building Indoor Anthrax Scenario

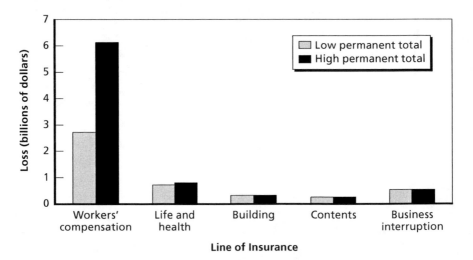

Figure A.14 shows the comparable results for the outdoor anthrax scenario. Unlike the indoor release case, the total insured losses are spread among several insurance lines in an outdoor release. Business interruption, building decontamination, and workers' compensation losses could exceed $30 billion each. The workers' compensation loss is 10 to 20 times higher than the $1.8 billion from the 9/11 attacks (Hartwig, 2004) and, as noted earlier, cannot be excluded from insurance coverage. The insurers maintain that the workers' compensation industry's capital is only $30 billion in its entirety (Hockman et al., 2004). With potential losses as large as $43 billion, they would argue that, without TRIA, their capital is grossly inadequate to back their workers' compensation line of business.

Decontamination of the many buildings within the large anthrax footprint would cost $33 billion, and decontamination and replacement of building contents would add another $23 billion, for a

Figure A.14
Distribution of Insured Losses Across Insurance Lines for the Outdoor Anthrax Attack in a Major Urban Area

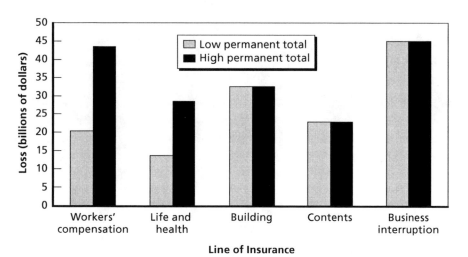

total of $56 billion.[16] Condemning buildings rather than decontaminating them would raise this value to over $200 billion.

Business interruption losses resulting from an outdoor anthrax release include only insured losses incurred by local businesses as a result of being closed in the aftermath of the attack, as discussed above. During the time that buildings have to be shutdown, the resultant business interruption losses would be $45 billion.

Again, with the CBRN exclusion generally specified in a property and casualty insurance policy (except workers' compensation) or if the CBRN coverage is not purchased, the property owner is not insured for this huge anthrax loss. The effect of terrorism insurance coverage take-up is discussed in detail in the main body of this study.

When we compared losses distinguished in terms of casualty (workers' compensation plus life and health) and non-casualty (building, contents, and business interruption), we found (as shown in Figure A.15) that casualty losses dominate in an indoor anthrax attack. The casualty loss ranges from $3.4 billion to $6.9 billion, far above the non-casualty loss of $1.1 billion. Even if the building must be condemned, the total property loss is $2.5 billion, which is still far less than the casualty loss.

Figure A.16 shows the losses in the outdoor anthrax scenario distinguished in terms of casualty and non-casualty losses. Unlike in the indoor case, the non-casualty loss would be larger than the casualty loss: The non-casualty loss is $100 billion, while the casualty loss ranges from $34 billion to $72 billion. When considering that actual property losses would be even greater than we estimate because our estimate does not include non-commercial property (see above) and because some buildings may have to be condemned rather than de-contaminated, the loss profile is even more skewed toward non-casualty losses.

---

[16] As discussed in Chapter Two, these building and contents values are minimum estimates because they cover commercial property only; the costs for decontamination and replacement in residential dwellings are not included.

Figure A.15
Comparison Between Casualty and Non-Casualty Losses for the Major Office Building Indoor Anthrax Scenario

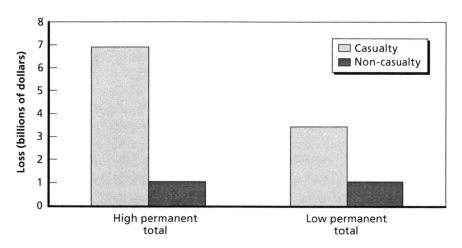

Figure A.16
Comparison Between Casualty and Non-Casualty Losses for the Outdoor Anthrax Scenario in a Major Urban Area

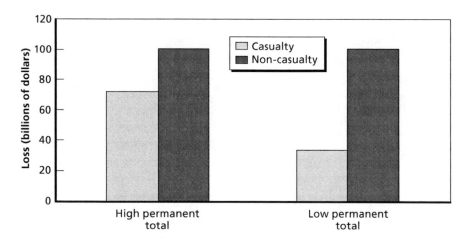

The RAND Anthrax Casualty Model and Casualty Distributions in the Indoor and Outdoor Anthrax Attacks

This appendix describes how we calculated the distribution of victims into various casualty categories resulting from exposure to anthrax. This model is an expanded version of one developed recently at RAND (Chow et al., n.d.) and includes the effects of not only anthrax infection but also antibiotic prophylaxes and medical treatments.

Inhalational anthrax is the form of anthrax that would result from the inhalation of anthrax spores. This form of the disease has three phases. The first phase is the incubation phase, where a person has inhaled the spores but does not yet show symptoms. The duration of this phase is variable. Prior to 1990, it was estimated to last between one and six days. Then analysis of the 1979 outbreak of inhalational anthrax in the Soviet city of Sverdlovsk indicated that it might last much longer—perhaps as long as 43 days. However, our recent analysis of the 2001 mail attacks in the United States has shown that this experience is incompatible with the Sverdlovsk data (Chow et al., n.d.). As a result of problems with the Soviet data, we prefer to base our estimate of the duration of the incubation phase on ten case histories from the United States, where the duration of the incubation phase is well known (eight of these cases are from 2001). The range of the duration from these ten cases is between one and six days (ironically the same range that had been estimated before the Sverdlovsk data had become available).

The second phase is the prodromal phase, which is the initial phase of the illness. Infected persons tend to show mild flu-like symptoms, which can be difficult to diagnosis as anthrax. We have collected 20 cases histories (none of which are based on the problematic Soviet data) where the untreated duration of the prodromal phase is known. The duration of this phase is also variable and can last from one to seven days.

The final phase is the terminal phase, which begins when the patient takes a sudden turn for the worse and dies generally within one to three days.

For our calculation of the numbers of ill and dead from inhalational anthrax, we use the case histories that we collected as the distributions of the duration of the incubation and prodromal phases (Chow et al., n.d.).[1] The durations of the incubation phase and the prodromal phase are uncorrelated.

For our analysis of the inhalational anthrax cases, we make the typical assumption that the median lethal dose is the inhalation of 8,000 spores. This means that half of those[2] who inhale this number of spores would become infected and the other half would not become infected, despite having inhaled this number of spores. To determine the fraction infected that would result from inhaling a number of spores that is different from 8,000, we use the methodology of Druett (1952). If one assumes that each spore acts independently to cause anthrax, then the fraction of people who are not infected (i.e., survivors) can be found by the expression $S = 0.5^D$ where D is the dose of spores expressed as a multiple of the median lethal dose. The fraction of those infected is then just $1 - S$. We assume that anyone who is infected and not treated will die.

Based on the results of the treatment of the inhalational anthrax victims of the 2001 anthrax mail attacks, we assume that all those who begin taking antibiotics in the incubation period will survive,

---

[1] With only ten cases for the incubation period, this distribution is not well specified, but unfortunately this is the best that can be done with the current state of knowledge.

[2] The general population (other than the military) is not vaccinated. Thus, we assume that the victims are not vaccinated beforehand.

regardless of how large a dose they may have inhaled. Similarly, we assume that 80 percent of those who are in the prodromal phase and are still at least one day away from becoming terminal can be saved by treatment. Such people will become seriously ill and require hospitalization and antibiotics to recover. People who are not treated until the terminal phase are assumed to die.

For the indoor base case, we calculated that the inhaled dose would be so high, regardless of the location of a victim inside the building, that every occupant would contract inhalational anthrax and therefore die if untreated. Effective counteractions occur at four days after the attack: three days to detect the attack and one day for effective counteractions to take place.

Using these assumptions and data, we then estimate the number of dead and ill using the distributions of the incubation and prodromal phases based on our collected case histories.

The number of dead from this attack is the sum of the following:

1. The number of dead on day four.
2. Those who are in the terminal phase of the disease on day four.
3. Those who would become terminal on day five.
4. Twenty percent of the remainder of those who are ill on day four and do not become terminal on day five.

Based on these assumptions and our distributions for the incubation period duration and the prodromal phase duration, we calculated that about 25 percent of the people in the building at the time of the attack die, 50 percent become ill but survive, and 25 percent never become ill. For our case of 10,000 occupants at the time of the attack, the above percentages translate into 2,500, 5,000, and 2,500, respectively.

However, there are three other sources of casualties and/or victims needing medical care in addition to those 10,000 people who are in the building at the time of the attack. First, since it will be three days before the attack is discovered, there will be people who were not in the buildings at the time of the attack but enter it after the attack and are exposed to re-aerosolized anthrax spores. Based on recent analysis, this could be a significant source of infection (Weis et al., 2002). However, there is no analytical way to estimate how many people might be infected in this way, and therefore we simply assume that this exposure increases the number of dead and the number of ill who recover by 10 percent. In other words, this adds 2.5 percentage points to the dead (i.e., 10 percent times 25 percent, or 250 persons), and 5 percentage points to the ill but recovered (i.e., 10 percent times 50 percent, or 500 persons).

Second, there will be people who were not in the building at the time of attack but enter it afterward and contract cutaneous anthrax.[3] The 11 cases of cutaneous anthrax that occurred as a result of the 2001 mail attacks show that this is a real concern. However, there is no analytical way to calculate the number of people who might contract cutaneous anthrax, and as a result we simply assume that this number equals 10 percent of the total number of people who were in the building at the time of the attack. Of the people who contract cutaneous anthrax, none die, 50 percent become ill enough to require hospitalization, and 50 percent become ill but can be treated on an outpatient basis with antibiotics (in the medical-only category). In other words, cutaneous anthrax patients add 5 percentage points distributed between the temporary-total- and the permanent-total-disability categories and 5 percentage points to the medical-only category (i.e., 10 percent times 50 percent, or 500 persons).

Third, there could be people who enter the building after the attack but would not receive enough exposure to become ill, or there could be people who think they were in the building at the time of attack but in fact were not. People in this third group would not require any antibiotics to avoid illness, but because of the severe consequences of becoming ill with anthrax, these people would have to take antibiotics anyway. We estimate that this number would be equal to those who were exposed in the initial attack and avoid illness

[3] Some could actually come in contact with spores that had settled on surfaces and as a result contract cutaneous anthrax disease.

because of prophylaxis, 25 percent of the 10,000 occupants (or 2,500 persons).

The RAND casualty model accepts the dose levels from the CONTAMW model or other models and calculates the casualties at various injury levels. We have used the classification scheme of RMS, which breaks the victims into six injury levels: medical only, temporary total disability, permanent partial disability—minor, permanent partial disability—major, permanent total disability, and fatal (although we have not populated the two permanent-partial categories). We place all victims taking antibiotics for illness prevention and not becoming ill in the medical-only category.

A major uncertainty is whether those who become ill enough to require hospitalization but survive will be permanently disabled or not. These people would include 100 percent of those who are ill with inhalational anthrax and 50 percent of those who get cutaneous anthrax; together, they number 6,000 in our case. There is very limited data available to resolve the uncertainty.

To deal with this uncertainty, we suggest using a "high-permanent-total-disability" case, where 75 percent of the ill who recover are in the permanent-total-disability category and 25 percent are in the temporary-total-disability category. We also suggest a "low-permanent-total-disability" case, where these percentages are reversed: 25 percent in permanent total disability and 75 percent in temporary total disability. We also consider the uncertainty to be too large to fine-tune the classification to populate the two other levels: permanent partial disability—minor and permanent partial disability—major). These results, along with the fractions for other injury levels, are summarized in Table B.1. Note the fractions add up to greater than one, since these fractions are based on the number of occupants at the time of attack (10,000) plus casualties among people who entered the building after the attack. In other words, the total number of people who need medical attention, including prophylaxis, is 14,250.

Table B.1
Casualty Distribution for an Indoor Anthrax Attack on a High-Rise Office Building (given as a fraction of the people in the building at the time of the attack)

Category	High-Permanent-Total Disability	Low-Permanent-Total Disability
Fatal	0.275	0.275
Permanent total disability	0.45	0.15
Temporary total disability	0.15	0.45
Medical only	0.55	0.55

For an outdoor anthrax attack, as was discussed in the text, we use the VLSTRACK model to calculate the outdoor dose that would be received at any location in the plume. This is then converted into an indoor dose by taking into account any dose reduction resulting from building ventilation systems. We then use the methodology of Druett (1952) to calculate the fraction of people who would be infected by this dose. As with the indoor attack, we assume that the attack is not discovered for three days and that it takes one more day before effective treatment can begin. As a result, new entrants to buildings in the contaminated area in the next few days after the attack but before detection would be infected by re-aerosolized anthrax spores or by direct contact with spores left on surfaces. These situations are similar to those that would occur in the indoor case. Thus, we assume that the relative proportions of temporary-total-disability, permanent-total-disability, and fatal casualties would be the same as those in an indoor attack. In other words, 27.5 percent of the infected population would be fatal; 15 percent/45 percent would be permanent total disability; and 45 percent/15 percent would be temporary total disability.[4]

As was discussed in the text, the number of medical-only casualties would be far greater and far more uncertain because of the need for very widespread antibiotic prophylaxis. In an indoor release, peo-

---

[4] The percentage before the slash is for the low-permanent-total-disability case, while the percentage after the slash is for the high-permanent-total-disability case.

ple potentially exposed to anthrax spores can be rather well identified, namely those in the building at the time of attack or thereafter until the attack is detected. In contrast, a person standing as far as 70 kilometers away from an outdoor anthrax release point can still have some chance (2 percent) of being infected. Uncertainties in wind direction, plume dispersion, and downwind travel distance lead to great uncertainty as to who might have been exposed. Thus, a very large number of people who were likely not exposed would have to be treated with antibiotics as a necessary precaution.

We bracket this uncertainty in the number of people requiring medical-only care by using two estimates. For the low estimate, we assume that all people in the actual plume footprint at the time of attack who are not in the three aforementioned casualty categories would be treated with antibiotics for prevention of illness. For the high estimate, we assume all the people in an area twice the size of the actual plume would need to take antibiotics; thus, we add these people to the medical-only category.[5] For this case then, the number of medical-only casualties would range from 1.0 to 1.9 million.

---

[5] The actual plume footprint is defined as the area receiving an anthrax dose that has a chance of greater than 2 percent to infect people if they are medically untreated. We further assume that the population densities in the neighboring areas are the same as those in the actual plume, except the highest density area (downtown) is replaced by that of the suburb density. In other words, the neighboring areas do not contain any more of the populous downtown, because the high density downtown has already been covered in the actual plume and accounted for.

Derivation of Equations (4.3) and (4.6)

Equation (4.3)

TRIA deductibles that would have been paid for WTC target insurers were estimated as

$$D_w^{eff} = Min\left(0.15 P_w^{TRIA}, L_w^{TRIA}\right),$$

where D_w^{eff} is the effective deductible for an individual WTC insurer, P_w^{TRIA} is the same insurer's annual direct-earned premium for TRIA-eligible insurance lines, and L_w^{TRIA} is the insurer's TRIA-covered loss at the WTC. The minimization is necessary because TRIA-covered losses were less than formal deductibles ($0.15\ P_w^{TRIA}$) for many WTC insurers. L_w^{TRIA} is approximated as

$$L_w^{total}\ P_w^{TRIA}\Big/P_w^{total},$$

where L_w^{total} is the insurer's total loss at the WTC and P_w^{total} is the insurer's total annual direct-earned premium. This relationship assumes that the fraction of coverage written by any insurer at the WTC that was TRIA-eligible was equal to the TRIA-eligible fraction written by that insurer nationwide. The ratio of aggregate TRIA deductible to TRIA-covered loss for the WTC was then computed as

$$D_{WTC}^{\mathit{eff}} \big/ L_{WTC}^{\mathit{TRIA}} = \sum D_{w}^{\mathit{eff}} \big/ \sum L_{w}^{\mathit{TRIA}} \,,$$

where the sums are over all primary insurers. Sums were calculated for primary insurer net loss only, because reinsurance is not TRIA-eligible. WTC insurer losses were taken from Schroeder, Saqi, and Winans (2002) and insurer direct-earned premiums for 2003 were taken from data provided by the National Association of Insurance Commissioners (Eric Nordman, personal communication with the authors, 2005).

Equation (4.6)

We assume that the portion of the loss in any event that is covered by insurers that also incurred a loss in the prior event is proportional to the fraction of the commercial property/casualty insurance industry's direct-earned premium represented by the insurers that incurred losses in that prior event:

$$L_{n,\in n-1}^{\mathit{TRIA}} = L_{n,total}^{\mathit{TRIA}} P_{n-1}^{\mathit{TRIA}} \big/ P_{total}^{\mathit{TRIA}} \,,$$

where $L_{n,\in n-1}^{\mathit{TRIA}}$ is the portion of the TRIA-covered loss in event n that is covered by insurers that also incurred a loss in event $n - 1$, $L_{n,total}^{\mathit{TRIA}}$ is the total TRIA-covered loss in event n, P_{n-1}^{TRIA} is the annual direct-earned premium on TRIA-eligible lines of the insurers incurring losses in event $n - 1$, and $P_{total}^{\mathit{TRIA}}$ is the total annual direct-earned premium on TRIA-eligible lines for the entire commercial property/casualty insurance industry. The loss that is covered by insurers who did not incur a loss in the prior event is then

$$L_{n,\notin n-1}^{\mathit{TRIA}} = L_{n,total}^{\mathit{TRIA}} \left(1 - P_{n-1}^{\mathit{TRIA}} \big/ P_{total}^{\mathit{TRIA}} \right).$$

For example, if insurers for one event comprised 15 percent of the commercial property/casualty insurance direct-earned premium, then, on average, 15 percent of the loss in the subsequent event would be incurred by duplicate insurers and 85 percent would be incurred by new insurers. This relationship can be extended to j multiple events to give:

$$L^{TRIA}_{n,\notin(n-1,n-2,\ldots n-j)} = L^{TRIA}_{n,total}\left(1 - P^{TRIA}_{n-1}\big/P^{TRIA}_{total}\right)\left(1 - P^{TRIA}_{n-2}\big/P^{TRIA}_{total}\right)\cdots$$
$$\left(1 - P^{TRIA}_{n-j}\big/P^{TRIA}_{total}\right),$$

$$\text{where } L^{TRIA}_{n,\notin(n-1,n-2,\ldots n-j)}$$

is the undeducted loss in event n. For events of the same size, L_n and P_n are constants that do not vary with n, so the relationship can be simplified to give:

$$L^{TRIA}_{n,\notin(n-1,n-2,\ldots n-j)} = L^{TRIA}_{n,total}\left(1 - P^{TRIA}_{n}\big/P^{TRIA}_{total}\right)^{n-1}.$$

If we continue to assume that the aggregate deductible for any event can be expressed in terms of the TRIA-covered loss, then we can use the relationship between the TRIA deductible and direct-earned premium, $D = 0.15P$, and Equation (4.3) to write

$$P^{TRIA}_{n} = \left(D^{eff}_{WTC}\big/L^{TRIA}_{WTC}\right)L^{TRIA}_{n,total}\big/0.15\text{, giving}$$

$$L^{TRIA}_{n,\notin(n-1,n-2,\ldots n-j)} = L^{TRIA}_{n,total}\left(1 - \frac{\left(D^{eff}_{WTC}\big/L^{TRIA}_{WTC}\right)L^{TRIA}_{n,total}}{0.15P^{TRIA}_{total}}\right)^{n-1}.$$

The aggregate deductible for event n is then computed from the undeducted loss by scaling to the WTC results as before:

$$D_n = \left(D_{WTC}^{eff} / L_{WTC}^{TRIA} \right) L_{n,total}^{TRIA} \left(1 - \frac{\left(D_{WTC}^{eff} / L_{WTC}^{TRIA} \right) L_{n,total}^{TRIA}}{0.15 P_{total}^{TRIA}} \right)^{n-1}.$$

The aggregate deductible for any cumulative loss made up of multiple events is then

$$D = \sum_{n=1}^{j} D_n,$$

where j is the number of events that generate that cumulative loss.

Bibliography

The 9/11 Commission Report, Final Report of the National Commission on Terrorist Attacks Upon the United States, 2004. Online at http://www. 9-11commission.gov/report/911Report.pdf (as of September 26, 2005).

Abernathy, Wayne A., Assistant Secretary of the Treasury, "Terrorism Risk Insurance Program," *Federal Register,* Vol. 68, No. 133, July 11, 2003, pp. 41250–41266. Online at http://www.treas.gov/offices/domestic-finance/financial-institution/terrorism-insurance/regulations/07_11_03. pdf (as of October 3, 2005).

Bauer, Timothy, and Roger Gibbs, *Software User's Manual for the Chemical/Biological Agent Vapor, Liquid, and Solid Tracking (VLSTRACK) Computer Model,* Version 3.1, Dahlgren, Va.: Dahlgren Division, Naval Surface Warfare Center, April 2001.

Bragg, J. S., *Terrorism Risk Insurance Program,* Presentation at the American Society of Workers' Compensation Professionals, June 21, 2005. Online at http://www.treas.gov/offices/domestic-finance/financial-institution/ terrorism-insurance/bragg06192005.ppt (as of September 26, 2005).

Centers for Disease Control and Prevention, *Strategic National Stockpile,* Atlanta, Ga.: CDC, April 14, 2005. Online at http://www.bt.cdc.gov/ stockpile/index.asp (as of September 26, 2005).

Chalk, Peter, Bruce Hoffman, Robert Reville, and Anna-Britt Kasupski, *Trends in Terrorism: Threats to the United States and the Future of the Terrorism Risk Insurance Act,* Santa Monica, Calif.: RAND Corporation, MG-393-CTRMP, 2005.

Chow, Brian, Gregory S. Jones, David Eisenman, and Tom LaTourrette, unpublished RAND research on bio-defense concepts of operations for the air force to administer prophylaxes and medical treatments, n.d.

Congressional Budget Office, *Federal Terrorism Reinsurance: An Update,* Washington, D.C.: Congressional Budget Office, January 2005. Online at http://www.cbo.gov/showdoc.cfm?index=6049&sequence=0 (as of October 3, 2005).

Dixon, Lloyd, John Arlington, Stephen J. Carroll, Darius Lakdawalla, Robert T. Reville, and David M. Adamson, *Issues and Options for Government Intervention in the Market for Terrorism Insurance,* Santa Monica, Calif.: RAND Corporation, OP-135-ICJ, 2004. Online only, http://www.rand.org/publications/OP/OP135/ (as of September 26, 2005).

Dixon, Lloyd, and Rachel Kaganoff Stern, *Compensation for Losses from the 9/11 Attacks,* Santa Monica, Calif.: RAND Corporation, MG-264-ICJ, 2004.

Doherty, N., E. Goldsmith, S. Harrington, P. Kleindorfer, H. Kunreuther, E. Michel-Kerjan, M. Pauly, I. Rosenthal, and P. Schmeidler, *TRIA and Beyond,* Philadelphia, Pa.: Wharton Risk Management and Decision Process Center, University of Pennsylvania, 2005. Online at http://grace.wharton.upenn.edu/risk/downloads/TRIA%20and%20Beyond.pdf (as of October 3, 2005).

Dols, W. Stuart, and George Walton, *CONTAMW 2.0 User Manual,* Washington, D.C.: National Institute of Standards and Technology, U.S. Department of Commerce, 2002.

Druett, H. A., "Bacterial Invasions," *Nature,* Vol. 170, 1952, p. 288.

Hartwig, R., *September 11, 2001: The First Year,* New York, N.Y.: Insurance Information Institute, 2002.

———, *2004 Mid-Year Property Casualty Insurance Update: Trends & Challenges in P/C Insurance Business Today,* New York, N.Y.: Insurance Information Institute, 2004. Online at http://www.iii.org/media/presentations/2004midyear/ (as of September 26, 2005).

Hockman, Bruce, Stephen Lowe, Samir Shah, and Charles Wolstein, *Workers Compensation Terrorism Reinsurance Pool Feasibility Study,* St. Louis, Mo.: Tillinghast-Towers Perrin, 2004. Online at http://www.towersperrin.com/tillinghast/publications/reports/WC_Terr_Pool/WC_Terr_Pool_Study.pdf (as of October 3, 2005).

Hubbard, R. G., and B. Deal, *The Economic Effects of Federal Participation in Terrorism Risk,* Analysis Group, 2004. Online at http://www.ag-inc.com/TRIA%20Report.pdf (as of September 26, 2005).

Jaffee, D. M., and T. Russell, *Should Governments Support the Private Terrorism Insurance Market?* paper prepared for WRIEC conference, Salt Lake City, Utah, August 2005. Online at http://faculty.haas.berkeley.edu/jaffee/Papers/DJTRSLCPaper.pdf (as of October 3, 2005).

National Institute of Standards and Technology (NIST), *Final Report of the National Construction Safety Team on the Collapses of the World Trade Center Towers* (draft for public comment), Washington, D.C.: U.S. Department of Commerce, 2005. Online at http://wtc.nist.gov/pubs/NISTNCSTAR1Draft.pdf (as of October 3, 2005).

Reissman, Dori B., et al., "One-Year Health Assessment of Adult Survivors of Bacillus anthracis Infection, *Journal of the American Medical Association,* Vol. 291, 2004, pp. 1994–1998.

Schroeder, Alice, Vinay Saqi, and Chris Winans, *Insurance and Risk Briefing,* New York, N.Y.: Morgan Stanley Equity Research, September 13, 2002.

Shane, Scott, "Anthrax Survivors Find Life a Struggle," *Baltimore Sun*, September 18, 2003.

Smetters, K., *Insuring Against Terrorism: The Policy Challenge,* working paper prepared for January 8–9, 2004, Conference of the Brookings–Wharton Papers on Financial Services, Philadelphia, Pa., 2004. Online at http://irm.wharton.upenn.edu/WP-Insuring-Smetters.pdf (as of September 26, 2005).

Snow, John W., "Treasury Releases Report on Terrorism Risk Insurance Act of 2002," letter sent by Treasury Secretary John W. Snow to Senate Banking Committee Chairman Richard Shelby and Ranking Member Paul Sarbanes and House Financial Services Committee Chairman Michael Oxley and Ranking Member Barney Frank, June 30, 2005. Online at http://www.treas.gov/press/releases/js2618.htm (as of October 3, 2005).

U.S. Department of the Treasury, *Assessment: The Terrorism Risk Insurance Act of 2002, Report to Congress,* Washington, D.C.: Office of Economic Policy, The U.S. Department of the Treasury, June 30, 2005. Online

at http://www.treas.gov/press/releases/reports/063005%20tria%20study.
pdf (as of September 26, 2005).

U.S. General Accounting Office, *Terrorism Insurance: Rising Uninsured Exposure to Attacks Heightens Potential Economic Vulnerabilities,* Washington, D.C.: U.S. General Accounting Office, GAO-02-472T, 2002. Online at http://www.gao.gov/new.items/d02472t.pdf (as of October 3, 2005).

Weis, Christopher P., et al., "Secondary Aerosolization of Viable *Bacillus anthracis* Spores in a Contaminated US Senate Office," *Journal of the American Medical Association,* Vol. 288, 2002, pp. 2853–2858.